W9-BNO-736

Praise for *Email Marketing Rules*

"This is a treasure trove of guidance for email marketers from an expert who has been covering retail email for years. It's clearly written, concrete and up-to-date. A must-have for any email marketer."

—Don Davis, Editor in Chief of
Internet Retailer Magazine

"I've followed Chad's columns for years and his book takes that accumulated knowledge and distills it into a must-read manual for any email marketer. Fantastic advice for creating a relevant program that will improve your email ROI."

—Aaron Oppliger, Email Marketing Specialist,
Oriental Trading Company

"This is, quite simply, the best book ever written about email marketing."

—Jay Baer, President of Convince & Convert,
Author of *Youtility*, and Co-Author of
The NOW Revolution

"The marketing books I enjoy most are those that can function as a continual reference for my day-to-day work. With its easy-to-reference segments, *Email Marketing Rules* will certainly serve this function for me—and my team, who have copies of their own—for a long time."

—Scott Cohen, Marketing Content Manager of
Western Governors University and email marketing
blogger on ScottWritesEverything.com.

"Chad is one of the top thought leaders in the email industry and *Email Marketing Rules* is a great book that lets the reader benefit from his deep insights and expertise. I recommend this book to anyone looking to gain a deeper understanding of the nuances of email marketing or as a refresher on what works and what doesn't in this often misunderstood marketing medium."

—Simms Jenkins, Founder & CEO of BrightWave Marketing and Author of *The New Inbox* and *The Truth About Email Marketing*

CHAD WHITE is an authority on email marketing trends and best practices, particularly within the retail industry, which he has covered for more than a decade as a journalist at Condé Nast and Dow Jones & Co. and as research director at the Direct Marketing Association, email marketing agency Smith-Harmon, and marketing software company Responsys. He's currently the principal of marketing research at ExactTarget, a global interactive marketing software provider.

Chad's research and commentary have appeared in more than 100 publications, including the New York Times, Wall Street Journal, USA Today, U.S. News & World Report, Ad Age, Adweek, MarketWatch and SmartMoney.

In addition to authoring "Email Marketing Rules," Chad has shared his insights and advice through thousands of blog posts and numerous research reports. He currently writes at EmailMarketingRules.com.

EMAIL MARKETING RULES

How to Wear a White Hat, Shoot Straight, and Win Hearts

Chad White

Foreword by Jay Baer

Email Marketing Rules: How to Wear a White Hat, Shoot
Straight, and Win Hearts
Copyright © Chad White, 2013

ISBN-13: 978-1484183304
ISBN-10: 1484183304

First Edition: March 2013

Warning and Disclaimer
Every effort has been made to the make this book as
complete and as accurate as possible, but no warranty or
fitness is implied. The information is provided is on an
"as is" basis. The author shall have neither liability nor
responsibility to any person or entity with respect to any
loss or damages arising from the information contained
in this book. The author is not a lawyer and none of the
information in this book shall be construed as legal
advice.

Acknowledgments

This book is the culmination of a thousand conversations. Some of those were live, via email, on Twitter, or through comments on my blog. Others were silent conversations I had by reading the articles, whitepapers and blog posts of my peers.

I am grateful for all the conversations I've had over the years, but I am especially grateful for those I had with Lisa Harmon, Jeff Rohrs, Loren McDonald, Morgan Stewart, Joel Book, Wacarra Yeomans, Simms Jenkins, David Daniels, DJ Waldow, Justine Jordan, Ros Hodgekiss, John Caldwell, Andrew Kordek, Anna Yeaman, Heather Goff, Dennis Dayman, Laura Atkins, Alex Williams, Linda Bustos, Justin Premick, Kelly Lorenz, Jordie van Rijn, Dela Quist, Tim Watson, Stefan Pollard, Stephanie Miller, Dylan Boyd and Jeanniey Mullen. Thank you for shaping, confirming and challenging my views.

For helping me complete this book, I'm exceedingly grateful to my amazing editors, Mark Brownlow and Aaron Smith, whose insights, guidance and suggestions were absolutely invaluable. Thanks also go to Kyle Lacy for designing the book cover, Andrea Smith for doing the illustrations, and to my long-time copyeditor, Alex Madison.

I'd also like to acknowledge Michael Pollan,

whose book *Food Rules* strongly influenced the format and style of my book (and perhaps influenced my choice of title as well).

But my most heartfelt thanks go to my wonderful wife, Kate, who supported and encouraged me during all the late nights spent writing this book and who inspired me to write it in the first place. Thanks, Love.

Contents

Glossary   **199**

Foreword

The Currency of Modern Marketing

By Jay Baer, President of Convince & Convert,
Author of *Youtility*, and Co-Author of
The NOW Revolution

This is, quite simply, the best book ever written about email marketing and I am honored and delighted to have been asked by Chad White—who perhaps knows more about the subject than anyone on the planet (and most assuredly has spent more time thinking about email than anyone on the planet)—to write the Foreword.

Email marketing is like driving a car. You have to learn how to do it, but once you've done so it's quite easy to take for granted. The litany of technology advances created by email service providers (ESPs) to make sending, tracking, targeting and automating email easier can make you feel like you're behind the wheel of a high-tech, luxury sports car. But successful email marketing—like all marketing, really—isn't about the car, it's about the driver.

Whether you're a new or casual email marketer

or a seasoned pro, you cannot take your hands off the wheel for a second. Just because you have remarkable technological horsepower at your disposal does not mean that your email program can or should run on auto-pilot. Yet, far too many are managed (or not managed) that way every day.

While the core underpinnings of email marketing haven't changed all that much in quite a while—you send an email, people receive it and hopefully open, read and click—what we know about email success, and how email works together with other communication modalities like social media, has increased considerably. And this, for me, is the most important aspect of this important book.

In *Email Marketing Rules*, you'll find a consistent thread woven throughout that is THE key insight about email marketing success—far more so than any best practice, or design guideline, or high-tech optimization technique. It's simply this: Email is a value exchange between a company and a person, and in a world where every one of us is being overtaken by an invitation avalanche with all companies of every size and description beseeching us to like, friend, follow, watch and click, the value provided by the company needs to steadily go up.

We've talked for years about the importance of permission in email marketing—about how to get new addresses, whether a double opt-in is a good idea, and how to manage unsubscribes. But the reality is that permission is a bottom of the funnel behavior that falls into the same category as a Facebook "like" and a Twitter "follow." It's simply the manifestation of something far more important...relevance.

It doesn't matter how special your offer is, or how beautiful your emails are, if your email marketing isn't truly and inherently relevant to people at a singular, personal level, you're in trouble, because relevance is the currency of modern marketing. What makes an effective Facebook post? Relevance (and resonance). What makes an effective tweet? Relevance. What makes an effective blog post? Relevance. The "What's in it for me?" calculation is being performed hundreds of times per day, across multiple channels, by every single one of your customers and prospects.

Permission is ephemeral. Opt-in isn't a lifetime Supreme Court appointment. Your ability to successfully email a person isn't static; it ebbs and flows based on circumstantial relevancy.

So as you read this remarkable book, take notes. Be thinking about how you can use these principles to increase relevancy. If you can devise and manage an email program that benefits subscribers first, the downstream benefits to the company will be astounding. Because ultimately, in this bouillabaisse of modern digital marketing, the smart companies create value, not just noise.

Introduction

*Unlock the Full Potential of Email
Marketing by Following Best Practices*

Email marketing's return on investment is
significantly higher than that for search and way
higher than the ROI of social media, mobile and
every other channel. While other channels excel at
raising awareness, customer acquisition and
fostering conversations, email marketing is THE
power channel for retention marketing. Consumers
strongly associate email marketing with deals and
product information, making it unrivaled at driving
sales and increasing loyalty.

But its impressive power obscures an
unfortunate truth:

Poor practices are blunting

email marketing's effectiveness

and keeping its ROI from

being truly awesome.

After many years of tracking the email
marketing campaigns of the largest retailers and

extensively researching their practices, I've never been more convinced that following best practices is the key to spectacular results. This book is about the practices that can take your email program to the next level, particular those that help you effectively connect with subscribers and win their loyalty. It's also about the "white hat" practices that will steer you clear of trouble, which is becoming an even stronger imperative.

It's a critical time for email marketing best practices. Despite all the talk about Big Data, analytics and performance-based decision-making, most budget allocations are based on gut feelings and internal politics because most businesses have only a rough idea of the returns generated by each of the channels they use.

Even in a channel like email, where there's above average visibility into program results, many companies don't know their ROI or the value of a subscriber. And even though testing is now quite easy to perform, most organizations don't make it a routine practice to determine the best approach to take.

Despite businesses typically having poor visibility into what works, there's a worrisome and growing trend of disparaging best practices.

Indeed, there appears to be a concerted effort to completely redefine what the term "best practice" even means. Best practices are not determined by what the majority does. The exception does not disprove the rule. And while it sounds snappy, the best practice is not "the practice that is best for your business," although often they are one and the same.

Best practices are those practices that generally produce the best results or minimize risk.

However, because every brand is different, with different circumstances and different audiences, it should be fully expected that some companies can successfully deviate from accepted industry best practices through experimentation. Instead of being a surprise or disproving best practices, such instances only serve to illustrate why testing is itself a best practice.

The truth is that while it's possible to test just about anything in email and that nearly everything is worth testing on some level, very few things actually get tested.

Given the reality of limited time and resources, best practices provide a valuable, low risk, default starting point.

That said, it's not always easy to identify a best practice, in part because the pace of change in the email marketing industry muddies the waters: Consumer behavior changes. The protocols of inbox providers change. Inbox capabilities change. Email-reading devices change. Email marketing capabilities change. Laws change.

Best practices bubble up from the innovators and leaders who are always experimenting and testing. They then become common practice as others are convinced of their merits. And finally, some become myths as the conditions that made them best practices change and companies are slow to adapt.

Indeed, it seems like there is no shortage of fallen best practices: "Never use special characters in your subject lines because they don't render properly." "Avoid using all-caps, exclamation marks and words like 'free' in your subject lines or your emails will be blocked." "Don't do anything to encourage unsubscribes." "Build your list from all possible sources because a bigger list is a more productive list."

The fall of certain best practices has led some to simplistically declare that "best practices are dead" rather than to acknowledge that we operate in a dynamic, evolving industry. But just because some best practices have died doesn't mean that all best practices are dead and that there aren't new best practices emerging all the time.

Following best practices doesn't make you mediocre, unimaginative

or a conformist.

Others have argued that "best practices are the pathway to mediocrity." That's ridiculously untrue for two reasons. First, not all marketers follow all best practices—not even close. So following best practices easily makes you solidly above average.

And second, most best practices allow for plenty of creative license in how exactly they are implemented, so there are lots of opportunities to express your unique brand and show off your marketing savvy and technological smarts. Think of best practices as a sheet of paper: It's confining only to the degree that you have to draw on the paper—and not on the table and floor and walls. So how well you execute best practices can elevate your program from above average to outstanding.

The war on best practices is particularly harmful to new practitioners, giving them the impression that anything goes.

The email marketing space is very fortunate to be experiencing rapid expansion, but that means many new people are coming into the industry with little to no experience. Marketing graduates rarely have much exposure to email marketing and many companies are building their email marketing teams with staffers who previously worked in the catalog and direct mail space, which has very different rules than email. Executives, who are vital partners in making email marketing successful, can also sometimes impede responsible and profitable decisions by being unfamiliar with email marketing's unique set of dynamic rules.

When newcomers hear "there are no rules," they inherently make assumptions based on their personal preferences, experiences, behaviors and tolerances. But taking a "focus group of one" approach or yielding to the highest paid person's opinion often leads to the wrong conclusions, especially for marketers and executives.

Marketers are very different from the average consumer, so your instincts may mislead you.

The chances are quite good that you have a lot less in common with your subscribers than you think. For instance, marketers are much more tech-savvy than the average person, are much more likely to own a smartphone, are more involved in social media, make more purchases online, and are less concerned about their privacy—to name just a few differences.

Rather than using your gut, it's wiser to start by following the conventional wisdom and then testing to see how your audience responds to incremental changes.

* * *

In this book I'll discuss two sets of rules. The first is *Fundamental Imperatives*, which are the 10 rules that are essential for all marketers to follow to the letter. These are the rules that separate legitimate marketers from spammers.

The second is *Practice Guidelines*, which are the rules that serve as the foundation for all of today's best practices. How these rules are translated into practice can vary from company to company, and some brands will discover through testing that they can bend or even break a few of these rules and achieve better results. These are the rules that separate great marketers from the pack.

The rules laid out on the following pages should endure all but the most radical changes in the email marketing ecosystem.

Although these rules are geared toward retailers and other consumer brands in the U.S., the vast majority of them also apply to business-to-business and international brands as well. I encourage you to share these rules with your colleagues, boss, business partners and new hires—anyone who has a hand in making your email program a success.

WORDS TO KNOW

---

permission
Actively or passively agreeing to receive promotional email

opt-in email marketing
Sending email only to those who have given you permission to do so

opt-out email marketing
Sending email to those who have not given you permission to do so and requiring them to unsubscribe or mark your emails as spam if they don't want to receive future emails

Controlling the Assault of Non-Solicited Pornography And Marketing Act of 2003 (CAN-SPAM)
A law regulating commercial email messaging that forbids deceptive messaging, requires senders to include a working unsubscribe link and their mailing address in every email they send, and requires senders to honor opt-out requests quickly, among other things

internet service provider (ISP)
Shorthand term for providers of web-based, desktop and mobile email inboxes that send, store and organize messages for users and manage and block spam (i.e., Gmail, Outlook, etc.)

email service provider (ESP)
A commercial provider of email marketing services that allows their clients to manage their email lists, send messages, track the response of message recipients, and process opt-ins and opt-outs, among other capabilities

---

sender reputation

A reflection of your trustworthiness as an email source that is affected by spam complaint rates and other factors that internet service providers use to determine whether to deliver, junk or block your email

---

Fundamental Imperatives

The Rules that Separate Legitimate Marketers from Spammers

For a long time, email has been caught between the opt-out marketing industry that's aligned with direct mail and the opt-in marketing industry that's aligned with mobile and social media.

Opt-out marketers have long argued for an expansive definition of permission and had a major victory in lobbying for the CAN-SPAM Act of 2003, which made opt-out the law of the land for email marketing. They had hoped the Act would perpetuate an anything goes, "Wild West" environment, but since then there has been a steady string of developments that have undermined opt-out email marketing—from changes in consumer behavior and internet service provider (ISP) practices to channel convergence and new foreign laws to data challenges around creating relevant messages.

ISPs have become so effective

at blocking malicious, traditional

spam that consumers now consider "spam" to be any unwanted or irrelevant email—even if it's from brands they know and even if they gave the brand permission to email them.

Being CAN-SPAM compliant is the legal low bar and provides absolutely no protection from having your emails junked or blocked by ISPs, which are the real lawmakers when it comes to email marketing. With ISPs deputizing and arming them with the lethal "report spam" button, consumers are zealous in reporting when they receive unwanted email. And wanting to keep their users happy, ISPs are diligent in listening to that feedback.

In recent years, ISPs have expanded their monitoring to include engagement metrics, such as opens and clicks, making it harmful to a brand's sender reputation to endlessly email non-responsive inboxes. Whereas you used to be able to stay in ISPs' good graces by having a low spam complaint rate, now you need to have a respectable percentage of your subscribers engaging with your messages as well.

With promotional email volume growing rapidly as brands shift their marketing efforts from traditional media to digital media like email, ISPs have also given their users new tools that give greater visibility to those emails from senders that are most important to them.

While opt-out marketers continue to struggle with the challenge of staying out of the junk folder, opt-in marketers are addressing the new challenge of earning entry into the portion of their subscribers' inboxes that's reserved for critical, must-read messages.

Many of the digital marketing channels that have risen to prominence after email are opt-in. The two biggest—social and mobile—are gradually converging with email.

In these new channels, consumers have total control. Marketers can't make consumers follow them on Pinterest or force their way onto a consumer's RSS reader, and SMS requires an opt-in by law—with some hefty penalties already handed out to lawbreakers. Permission is fundamental to these channels and can be given and taken away at will, with no recourse for the marketer.

The control that consumers have over these new channels is increasing the expectation of control that they have when using email. And that sense of entitlement is growing as email converges with social media and mobile as we head toward a "unified inbox" where emails, texts, voicemail and other messages are comingled. The inbox is becoming a much more personal space as email increasingly migrates from desktops and laptops to tablets and smartphones, which consumers carry with them everywhere.

> **Other countries have enacted marketing laws that have an opt-in mandate, and the jurisdictions of these countries' laws can be quite expansive.**

The marketing laws of foreign countries—and in particular, of Canada, the U.K. and Europe—stand in sharp contrast to those of the U.S. While the CAN-SPAM Act focused on the worst malicious and deceptive spammers, the laws elsewhere recognize that consumers also deserve protection from unwanted emails from legitimate marketers.

While there's no chance of CAN-SPAM being revisited in the near future, U.S. marketers may find that the marketing laws of other countries apply to them because of where subscribers live or where subscribers are travelling when they check their email. Especially for global companies, the risk of not practicing permission-based email marketing is rising.

The central reason that ISPs and lawmakers have moved so aggressively to protect inboxes is that the incremental cost to send an email is nearly zero. In contrast, the advertising costs associated with traditional channels like TV, print and direct mail ensure that marketers use those channels thoughtfully.

With email marketing, recipients and ISPs bear the vast majority of the cost of the marketing—recipients in terms of time and attention, and ISPs in terms of infrastructure and other costs.

It's a critical difference. While those traditional channels are paid channels, email marketing is largely an earned channel. Marketers earn access to inboxes through permission and maintain it by sending valuable emails.

Rejecting this fundamental truth and treating email like a paid or owned channel—like spammers do—causes consumers to report your email as spam, which in turn causes ISPs to junk or block your email. And once you're blacklisted, the effort you spend crafting your messages is all for naught, as most of the intended recipients will never see it.

Permission takes effort to obtain, which is why spammers and some legitimate brands skip this step of the relationship-building process. Even though it's the equivalent of bursting into someone's house without being invited, some marketers believe their message is so compelling that their trespassing will be forgiven.

Permission is a pre-condition of creating relevance.

Many marketers with strong permission practices and data on past purchases, click behavior and preferences struggle to consistently create relevant messages and remain welcome in their subscribers' inboxes. So the idea that a company without permission could collect, purchase, harvest or steal enough information to consistently create messages relevant enough to trump the need for permission is simply arrogant and delusional. Consumer expectations are just too high and ISP vigilance too unforgiving at this point.

Spending time pursuing unethical and unwise practices is time spent away from using proven methods to build a successful program.

Just because a practice is legal or established companies provide a service doesn't mean that the practice or service is ethical, wise or likely to be profitable for you. The "satisfied customers" of such services likely have poor visibility into the performance of their email marketing programs and just aren't accounting for the negative impact of their practices. When all the negatives—such as sender reputation damage and brand damage—are factored in, the return on investment of these unethical practices and services becomes minimal or even negative.

Your time is much better spent trying to attract new subscribers by selling them on the benefits of your program and earning their permission, which is the focus of the first 10 rules.

WORDS TO KNOW

passive consent
Permission indicated when a person does not act to keep you from adding them to your email list (i.e., not unchecking pre-checked box)

active consent
Permission indicated when a person explicitly acts to indicate that they want you to add them to your email list (i.e., checking unchecked box)

unsubscribe process
How subscribers remove themselves from your email list

opt-out page
Webpage that is launched when subscribers click the "unsubscribe" link in your emails and allows subscribers to complete the unsubscribe process

spamtrap or honeypot
Sending email to these long-abandoned or uncirculated email addresses causes ISPs to label you a spammer and block your email

inactive subscriber
A subscriber who has not opened or clicked in any of your emails in a long time; the opposite of an active or engaged subscriber

list rental
Having a message sent on your behalf to an email list owned by someone else

The Law

1

Follow the law, but recognize that doing so gives you no protection from spam complaints or being blocked by ISPs.

In the U.S., the Controlling the Assault of Non-Solicited Pornography And Marketing Act of 2003 (CAN-SPAM) is the primary law regulating commercial email messaging and it sets a very low bar for acceptable behavior. In fact, it sets the bar so low that legitimate email marketers should be much more concerned about getting into trouble with ISPs than with the federal government.

CAN-SPAM makes a few demands of email marketers: You must include a working unsubscribe link in every promotional email and honor opt-out requests quickly. And you must include your mailing address in every email you send and never use misleading or deceptive sender names, subject lines or email copy, or attempt to conceal your identity or the fact that you're sending advertising.

Besides violating CAN-SPAM, these tactics erode subscriber trust and lead to unsubscribes and spam complaints. Recognize that misrepresenting who the sender is or falsely using "Re:" or "Fwd:" in a subject line, for instance, is not a marketing gimmick or tactic; it is a lie—and potentially a crime.

Depending on your target audience and countries of operation, your email program may be subject to other marketing laws. Please consult an attorney to determine your risks.

Permission

2

Make sure consumers are aware that you are adding them to your email list.

If consumers are unaware that you've opted them into your email program, then they didn't give you permission. Hiding permission consents in your "Terms and Conditions," "Privacy Policy," or sweepstakes or contest rules is wholly insufficient. It's well established that consumers don't read privacy policies or terms and conditions. Besides, such consents don't protect you from spam complaints and will get you no sympathy from an internet service provider's abuse desk staff.

While using a prominently positioned and clearly worded pre-checked box of adequate size can make a consumer aware that they are opting in if they take no action, permission is strongest when actively given—whether it is by checking a box or completing a sign-up form explicitly to receive email.

Permission

3

Never make an email opt-in mandatory for a customer interaction.

You can't force consumers to give you permission to send them promotional emails in exchange for the right to register a product, receive a receipt via email, enter a contest or anything else. Doing so will cause some consumers to abandon the interaction while forcing the rest to unsubscribe or mark your email as spam when they receive it. Instead, use the interaction as an opportunity to sell them on the value of becoming an email subscriber.

Permission

4

Make unsubscribing easy, taking no more than two clicks, and honor opt-out requests immediately.

Your unsubscribe process is competing against the one-click, never-fail "report spam" button, so it's in your best interest to make opting out as friction-free as possible to avoid spam complaints.

The unsubscribe link needs to be easy to find upon scanning your promotional emails, so small text and light grey fonts on white backgrounds should be avoided. Use white space, bold text and other typographical elements to make it stand out.

The unsubscribe link should never appear only in the form of graphical text or an image-based button because it would not be displayed if images were blocked. It's best if the link text is the word "Unsubscribe" or a phrase that starts with that word, such as "Unsubscribe or Change Your Email Address" or "Unsubscribe or Update Your Email Preferences," as consumers have been trained to look for that keyword. Avoid a generic "click here" for your unsubscribe link.

If you include an unsubscribe link at the top of your emails, you should also include one in your footer, as subscribers are used to looking for it there.

The unsubscribe process itself should consist of no more than two clicks—one on the unsubscribe link in the email and one on the opt-out page. Requiring subscribers to login to access your unsubscribe page drives up spam complaints. It's illegal to require anything besides the subscriber's email address to process an opt-out request.

While the CAN-SPAM Act stipulates that you have up to 10 business days to process opt-outs, this regulation should not be interpreted as a green light to continue to email consumers who have just unsubscribed. That window was permitted solely to provide large companies with lots of independent agents the necessary time to suppress every instance of an address from their email lists.

Even if your company fits this description, technology has improved drastically since CAN-SPAM was passed. Any legitimate email service provider (ESP) will be able to process your opt-outs as they happen.

Regardless of what's legal, consumers that continue to receive emails from you after opting out are increasingly likely to report your emails as spam, in addition to thinking less of your brand because of the annoyance.

Remember that just because a consumer wants to stop receiving emails from you doesn't mean that they will stop buying from you or will stop interacting with you through other channels. Don't risk damaging a consumer's relationship with your brand by refusing to gracefully accept their desire

to end their email relationship with your brand for
the time being.

Permission

5

Accept that permission expires.

People find new hobbies, discover new brands they prefer more, go up- or down-market because of changing finances, change jobs, and move to new cities or neighborhoods. Subscribers lose interest in your emails for a variety of reasons, some of which have nothing to do with the content of your emails or even your brand. And even though they no longer want your emails, some subscribers will just never bother to unsubscribe.

Your emails also may not reach a subscriber for technical or logistical reasons, such as your emails being junked or filtered into a folder that they never check or the subscriber abandoning their email address all together.

At a certain point, the reason doesn't matter. When a subscriber hasn't opened or clicked in a single email for a prolonged period of time, it's up to you to recognize that their silence means permission has been withdrawn.

Individual brands can determine for themselves how long a subscriber can be inactive before they stop sending emails to them based on the impact on their sender reputation. However, a good rule of thumb is to stop mailing or at least dramatically reduce the frequency of mailings to subscribers who have been inactive for 13 months or longer, a time period that takes into consideration once-a-year buyers. And definitely do not send any mail to subscribers who have been inactive for 25 months or longer. High-frequency senders like daily deal sites may find that they need to take action when a subscriber has been inactive for just a few months to avoid negative consequences.

One important caveat to this is new subscribers. If someone hasn't opened or clicked any of your emails during their first 30 days on your list, you should investigate to see if your emails are being blocked by the subscriber's ISP or some other issue is keeping the subscriber from getting your emails. But if you don't uncover any delivery problems, you should stop mailing them.

Permission

6

Accept that knowing one of your customer's email addresses doesn't constitute permission to reach them at any of their other email addresses.

So-called email change of address (ECOA) and other services that provide a consumer's other email addresses are a violation of privacy and do not constitute permission.

Most consumers maintain multiple email addresses, using each one for different purposes. Consumers also abandon email addresses for various reasons. Using ECOA and other services to force your way into your subscribers' other inboxes because you're unhappy with the one you were allowed entry to—even if you believe the address has been abandoned—is disrespectful and a violation of privacy.

Permission

7

Accept that securing an opt-in to another channel doesn't constitute permission to reach a consumer via email as well.

Knowing a customer's mailing address or phone number, or connecting with them on Facebook, LinkedIn or other social network doesn't constitute having permission to add the customer to your email list. Doing an email address append (e-append) or scraping an email address off a contact's profile page for mass marketing purposes is invasive and heavy-handed and is not how to build the foundation for a positive, profitable relationship.

If you have the means to reach a customer through another channel, use that to explicitly ask the customer for permission to reach them via email as well.

Permission

8

Don't share email addresses with other brands within your company.

Just because a consumer opts in to receive emails from one of your brands doesn't mean that they're interested in getting emails from your other brands. Consumers may not be aware of your other brands and, if they are, probably aren't aware that they are part of the same parent company. To protect yourself from souring the existing brand relationship, each of your sister brands must secure its own email permission.

The good news is that you can leverage one brand relationship to expose subscribers to your other brands and get additional opt-ins. Your opt-in confirmation page, welcome email series, preference center and promotional emails can all be used to educate subscribers about your other brands and give them the chance to opt in to their email programs.

Permission

9

Don't buy email lists or barter for email addresses.

Very few consumers knowingly give a company permission to sell their email address to other companies. So if you purchase an email list, at best you'll reach inboxes that are overrun with marketing messages and spam. But more than likely you'll reach spamtraps, abandoned email addresses, and unsuspecting and unreceptive people whose email addresses were scraped from the web and who are almost guaranteed to mark your emails as spam.

Sending email to a purchased email list is a quick and easy way to ruin your sender reputation and get you blocked by major ISPs. Reputable ESPs will fire clients found using purchased lists.

Permission

10

When renting an email list, the list owner should never share the list with the renter.

If you rent a list from a company, you should supply the company with the message that you want sent. The list owner then sends that message on your behalf to their list—which you never see— using their usual name and email address, not yours. The unsubscribe link included in this email is an opt-out for the list owner only, not you. The list owner typically includes a message at the top of the email indicating that the message is from one of their partners.

This arrangement helps ensure that your message will be well received by the recipients, because the list owner would suffer unsubscribes and spam complaints if they sent a message from a partner that wasn't a good fit for their list.

List providers that are unwilling to follow this procedure should be viewed with great skepticism, as it's a sign that they either don't have permission to contact the people on their list or that the list is a poor match for your brand.

The message you send to a rented list should ideally give you the chance to convert the recipients into registered customers or into subscribers of your own. Those that opt in are now your subscribers and there's no need to rent those email addresses again.

The Last Word on Fundamental Imperatives

The Permission Rule

Besides the first Fundamental Imperative, which puts you on the right side of the law, the other rules focus on permission, because permission really is the foundation of the email marketing relationship. And in the minds of consumers, there's no clearer or more immediate marker of a spammer than violating permission.

Condensing rules 2 through 9 gives us *The Permission Rule*:

Permission is consciously and willingly given, email address–specific, channel-specific, brand-specific and temporary.

Simply by taking the time to earn a consumer's permission and respecting the limits of that opt-in, you've taken a huge step toward fostering the trust necessary to build a profitable email relationship, as well as safeguarding your sender reputation, protecting yourself from excessive spam complaints, and ensuring your deliverability remains high.

A strong focus on permission also puts you in a customer service frame of mind that's vital to achieving stellar email marketing performance—which is the subject of the remainder of this book.

WORDS TO KNOW

owned media
Marketing channels that a brand owns, such as their website, blog and mobile app

paid media
Marketing channels that a brand pays to have access to, such as TV, radio, magazines, newspapers, billboards, paid search and display ads

leased media
Marketing channels that a brand has free access to but doesn't control, such as Facebook, Twitter and Pinterest

earned media
Marketing channels that a brand earns access to, such as word of mouth and publicity

relevance
How valuable a subscriber thinks your emails are over time—which is largely determined by how many emails you send, when they arrive, their content, and how they look and function within whichever email reader is being used

Practice Guidelines

The Rules that Separate Great Marketers from Good Marketers

Many marketers think about their email list as something they own. Some quietly sell their list to brokers, who quietly resell that list to others. Some bankrupt companies have very publicly sold their list while liquidating their assets. And a few companies have been valued largely based on the size of their list. But despite these occurrences,

lists are owned only to the extent that someone can own a collection of handshake agreements that can be cancelled at any time for any reason.

The truth is that email users, empowered by ISPs, own the email channel and that marketers earn the right to use the email channel by meeting or exceeding subscribers' expectations.

Marketers set expectations during the signup process by how they attract subscribers, the information they require from subscribers, the content they say they'll send and how frequently they say they'll send it. But once permission is obtained, email marketing then becomes all about living up to the continually rising expectations of subscribers.

While permission earns marketers access to inboxes, sending relevant messaging maintains that permission.

Relevance means sending subscribers emails they routinely find valuable or engaging. The content of the emails, how frequently they are sent, and how the emails display on the subscriber's email reader of choice are all factors in relevance.

Of course, relevance is in the eye of the beholder, so it's critical to listen to subscribers by monitoring how they interact with your emails and then respond appropriately.

When you don't, many subscribers will decide your emails "aren't relevant" and your email frequency is "too much." Those are consistently the top two reasons given by subscribers for leaving email lists, either via the unsubscribe link or the never-fail "report spam" button, depending in part on how much trust the email program has established.

Your subscribers' time is far more

valuable than the pittance it costs you to email them. It's that cost-value gap that relevance has to fill.

All marketers should feel pressure to boost the relevance of their email programs. Leading email marketers invest in more data analytics for targeting and personalization, more automation for triggered messages, and more design and coding resources to increase the functionality and user-friendliness of their emails. That is in turn raising subscribers' expectations.

At the same time, ISPs and other tool providers are adding functionality to help email users separate really important email from the other messages received—whether it's flagging emails from your contacts or filtering marketing messages into a special folder.

While staying out of the junk folder was the challenge of the past decade, the challenge of this decade is to earn entry into the must-read portion of subscribers' inboxes.

Relevance is the key to succeeding in this new environment and creating relevance is a major focus of the remaining rules, which cover everything from measuring program success and building a productive list to email design and testing.

The Practice Guidelines discussed hereafter are not an absolute answer to what you should do, but rather provide strong directional guidance. It's up to you to decide how best to work within the guidelines as best suit your organization.

Program Success

Most CEOs could care less about what your open and click rates are. While such metrics are important secondary indicators of program health, CEOs want to know how the email program is helping the business succeed. For most brands, success is quantifiable in terms of the revenue generated by the email program, the revenue growth rate, and other revenue-focused metrics such as average order size and lifetime value.

WORDS TO KNOW

---

email metrics
Measurements of the effectiveness of your email marketing program

open
When a subscriber views an email with images enabled

click
When a subscriber selects a link or linked image in an email and visits the associated webpage

conversion
When a subscriber clicks through an email and then makes a purchase, registers for an event, or takes another action requested by the email

subscriber lifetime value
The cumulative revenue generated by a subscriber during their time on your list

---

Program Success

11

Focus on maximizing the value of a subscriber, not on maximizing the results of a campaign.

Every company faces pressure to maximize short-term results; however, the ultimate goal of every business should be to maximize long-term results. In email marketing, that means looking at the lifetime value of a subscriber rather than per-campaign results, which can be deceptive.

This approach looks at the cumulative effect of your email marketing efforts on your subscribers. And while it puts the focus on revenue, it also recognizes that campaigns and content that keep subscribers engaged and primed to convert in the future are also valuable and contribute to revenue indirectly.

This approach also acknowledges that content, gimmicks and tricks that diminish trust, lower engagement, or increase unsubscribes and spam complaints are to be minimized because they diminish lifetime value.

As an alternative to lifetime value, you might consider looking at your subscribers' behavior over a period of time by using open reach, click reach and conversion reach metrics. For instance, measuring your click reach over the past quarter would mean measuring the percentage of your subscribers that clicked at least once during that time.

The key is to avoid a campaign-by-campaign mentality when looking at data, because that can cause you to misunderstand how subscribers are reacting to your overall messaging and to unintentionally make campaign-specific decisions that reduce the overall effectiveness of your email program.

Program Success

12

Measure your negative performance metrics, not just your positive ones.

When evaluating strategies and tactics, make sure you're seeing the whole picture by measuring negative metrics such as unsubscribes and spam complaints—and perhaps even negative social media chatter, word of mouth and other indications of brand impression.

It's tempting to want to turn a blind eye to negative indicators, especially when the positive ones are high, but negatives should be minimized because they can diminish the success of your future campaigns.

Program Success

13

Recognize that many of the actions prompted by emails are not easily trackable.

While it is more quantifiable than most other channels, email is not nearly as measureable as it's often portrayed. That's because subscribers often respond to emails in ways that are untrackable.

For instance, some subscribers will type in the URL of your site into their browser or search for your brand on a social media site rather than clicking though an email. Others will visit your store or event offline after seeing it promoted in an email. Some use one email address to subscribe to promotional emails and another account when making purchases. Still others will forward an email to their spouse or to friends, who will take action. And then there's word of mouth and social sharing.

Depending on your audience and business model, more than 50% of your email response may not be readily apparent.

Using promo codes that are unique to a particular subscriber and promoting printable and mobile coupons—particularly if those are also trackable back to individual subscribers—are a couple of ways to help measure the pass-along and offline influence of email.

An even better way is to do a "withhold study," where you don't send promotional emails to a group of subscribers for a while and then compare their activity to subscribers who received emails. This approach provides insights into the incremental sales influenced solely by email while also filtering out sales attributed to email that would have happened anyway.

Program Success

14

Don't attach too much meaning to your open rates.

The open rate is really a misnomer, as it doesn't accurately reflect the percent of recipients that opened your email. An open is registered only if a recipient views an email with images enabled. So if images are blocked, no open is recorded, even if the recipient reads the email top to bottom. Since blocking images is fairly common, open rates can be quite misleading.

But more importantly, opens are of marginal use as a success metric because generating opens is rarely the primary goal of a campaign and lots of opens doesn't necessarily translate into lots of sales.

Program Success

15

Benchmark yourself primarily against yourself.

Everyone wants to know how their email program stacks up against others, but external benchmarks are of little use for a number of reasons.

First, most aggregations of data are not going to be relevant to your industry or company. Even if the benchmark is for your industry, it's impossible to account for differences between companies of different sizes and that operate within different sub-verticals.

Second, the open rate and click rate data that is typically shared may not be very useful. Because brands manage their lists differently, these numbers don't provide an apples-to-apple comparison.

And third, beating an external benchmark can give you a false sense of security and make you complacent when you shouldn't be.

All of that said, if you are massively trailing external benchmarks, changes may be needed. Otherwise, focus on systematically beating your own performance.

Deliverability

Your sender reputation and the percentage of your emails that make it to your subscribers' inboxes are mostly a reflection of your permission practices, although your signup processes and other factors can also come into play.

WORDS TO KNOW
_____

deliverability
Getting your emails delivered to your subscribers' inboxes, as opposed to blocked or junked

bounced
When email is rejected by an internet service provider because it was sent to an unknown email address (hard bounce) or because of a temporary condition like the recipient's mailbox being full (soft bounce)

throttling
When an internet service provider slows the rate at which they deliver a sender's emails to their users

junked or bulked
When emails are routed to a recipient's "junk" or "spam" folder by an ISP

blocked
When emails are not delivered by an ISP

blacklist
A list of senders of spam typically maintained by an

independent organization that is used by ISPs in determining whether and where to deliver email

content filtering

When an ISP evaluates an email's subject line and other content as part of its process to decide whether and where the mail should be delivered

---

Deliverability

16

Use an email service provider to send your commercial email.

The technical issues around sending commercial email is now complicated enough that using anything less than professional-grade software is very risky and using homegrown software is unwise for all but the most sophisticated companies.

In addition to providing analytics, targeting, testing and other functionality, email service providers (ESPs) handle many issues that impact your deliverability, such as removing email addresses that hard bounce, monitoring feedback loops and removing complainers, setting up servers properly, sending emails at a rate that's acceptable to each ISP, and helping you determine whether a shared or dedicated IP address is best for you.

Thankfully, no matter how small or large your email needs are or what industry you're in, there are many ESPs available to choose from.

Deliverability

17

Accept that ESPs have relatively little control over the deliverability of your emails.

While using an ESP certainly helps your deliverability, the most critical factor impacting whether your emails reach your subscribers' inboxes is your sender reputation, which is a direct consequence of your permission practices, expectation setting, email frequency, how relevant your subscribers think your emails are, and how you handle subscribers who are no longer engaging with your emails.

All of those factors will determine whether your sends generate too many bounces from bad email addresses, too many spam complaints, and too little engagement in terms of opens and clicks, forcing ISPs to throttle, junk or block your emails.

Another source of deliverability problems is incorrectly entered email addresses, whether it's a typo made by the subscriber or a verbal transcription error made by a store associate or call center representative. Sometimes these errors can lead to spamtraps getting onto your list. Since ISPs and blacklisting organizations use these long-abandoned or uncirculated email addresses to identify spammers, having even one spamtrap on your list can seriously affect your deliverability.

Process improvements can address these issues, like having subscribers enter their email address twice and allowing store customers to visually verify that the store associate collected their address accurately. You might also consider tools that identify common misspellings like "someone@hotmali.com" or "someone@aol.ocm."

Deliverability

18

Don't obsess over content filtering when writing subject lines and creating email content.

Nowadays your subject lines and the words and images in your emails are given very little weight when ISPs determine whether to deliver your emails. Using exclamation marks, all caps, and words like "free" and "offer" in your subject lines will not affect your deliverability unless you have other factors seriously affecting your sender reputation.

That said, corporate email filters may give more weight to subject lines and email content, so business-to-business email marketers face some additional uncertainties that business-to-consumer email marketers don't have to worry about as much. Content scoring tools exist that can help you identify some potential problems.

List Building

Locating the best sources of quality subscribers and creating a subscription process that's as friction-free as possible are key to building a productive, low-risk email list.

WORDS TO KNOW

---

list building
The process of adding email addresses to your mailing list

email acquisition source
The form or mechanism through which a subscriber opts in, or the ad, sign or other vehicle that causes them to opt in

confirmed or double opt-in
The process of sending an email to a new subscriber that requires them to click on a link in the email to confirm their signup or else receive no additional emails

opt-in confirmation page
Webpage or messaging that follows a successful email signup

preference center
Webpage that displays a subscriber's email address and other details, such as profile information (zip code, etc.) and communication preferences (topics of interest, etc.), and allows them to make changes as well as unsubscribe

progressive profiling

Collecting additional demographic data and information about interests from subscribers by periodically asking them questions via email

---

List Building

19

Recognize that all subscribers are not equally valuable or desirable.

The expectations of your subscribers—and therefore, their value—can be very different depending on where and why they opt in. Tracking the performance of your subscribers by their acquisition source will allow you to see how each is performing and make decisions about which sources to continue, improve or abandon.

Email addresses can be acquired through many sources, including via your website, your store checkout, your blog, a signup request on product packaging or a receipt, an SMS text-to-subscribe sign, your Facebook page, a sweepstakes or contest entry form, co-registration on someone else's website, and on and on.

List Building

20

Focus on adding engaged subscribers to your list.

Growing your list expands the reach of your messages only if you're adding engaged subscribers. Adding low-quality subscribers to your list who are more likely to ignore or "junk" your emails than open and act on them is worse than pointless. It's counterproductive.

Lists that generate too many spam complaints and are bloated with unengaged subscribers tend to have deliverability problems—that is, their emails are diverted to junk folders or blocked altogether by one or more ISPs. In addition to costing time and effort to correct, deliverability problems mean that your emails aren't reaching even your engaged subscribers.

Unqualified list growth is a poor goal and worse key performance indicator. "Engaged list growth," where list size is grown while maintaining or expanding the percentage of engaged subscribers, is a much more effective and safer goal.

List Building

21

Recognize that the best email acquisition sources are always those that are closest to your shopping and customer service operations.

People who are on your website, buying your products, shopping at your stores, and talking to your service reps are more familiar with and interested in your brand than those who haven't done those things. That naturally makes such people higher value and less risky subscribers, and that makes your website, online checkout, store checkout, product packaging and call centers the best email acquisition sources.

Subscriber quality declines and the risk of spam complaints rises the farther you get away from these operations. Signups that come from sources outside of your business—such as list rentals and co-registrations—are among the least valuable and most prone to generating spam complaints, but even your social channels can produce subpar subscribers.

List Building

22

Use confirmed opt-in to protect yourself from low-quality email acquisition sources.

When using email acquisition sources that are outside of your organization or sources that have proven to produce low-quality subscribers, using a confirmed opt-in process can protect your list quality from slipping.

This involves sending an email to a new subscriber that requires them to click to confirm their signup. If they don't confirm, then they receive no additional emails. This ensures that you're adding active email addresses and subscribers who have a genuine interest in receiving your emails.

While call center email signups generate quality subscribers, recording email addresses can be prone to errors because of verbal transcription errors. In-store signup can be equally troublesome because of misread handwriting, although having the consumer enter their email address themselves on a tablet or kiosk can fix this issue. A confirmed opt-in process may be warranted in these situations and others depending on your process.

Confirmed opt-in may also be desirable when

you want proof that the address owner signed up, which might be necessary in certain cases such as when minors are involved.

List Building

23

Don't force people to register as a customer in order to receive promotional emails from you.

The word "Register" conjures up visions of long, over-reaching forms and troublesome site passwords in the minds of consumers—and the reward for registering is highly inconsistent. So don't hide your email signup on a customer registration form. Break it out into a separate form that you highlight on your homepage and throughout your website.

Signing up for email is a lower bar than customer registration, but if you treat these subscribers well and demonstrate your value then over time, you can get the same information from them as someone who registered.

List Building

24

Make your email signup requests and forms prominent to boost their performance.

Opt-in forms and links convert better when prominently placed high on your website where visitors don't have to scroll to find them. Consumers have been trained to expect to find them in the upper and lower right-hand corners of your webpages, so placing them there should also boost performance. Place them on every page of your website to increase signups.

Lightboxes, popovers and other in-your-face signup requests can also be effective, but be aware that some visitors may be annoyed by these, especially if they are forced to view them repeatedly. So it's important to test when and how often they are displayed to optimize the overall impact.

List Building

25

Tell consumers why they should sign up to receive your emails.

No one wants to join a list, get your emails, or receive your newsletter. But people do want to receive discounts, product updates, helpful advice and company news.

So be sure to sell people on the benefits of subscribing to your email program—whether you have the space to lay out the comprehensive benefits along with images or links to sample emails, or whether you only have space for 30 characters.

List Building

26

Avoid using overly rich signup incentives because they can attract low-quality subscribers.

Some consumers will subscribe to your emails just for the signup incentive and then turn around and unsubscribe or report your email as spam.

One approach to mitigating this risk is to keep sign-up incentives to a moderate value or ensure that the incentive is only attractive to loyal customers. Another approach is simply to avoid signup incentives all together to make certain that people are subscribing solely because they want your emails.

Not promoting a signup incentive doesn't mean you can't provide a reward for subscribing in a welcome email.

List Building

27

Deliver signup incentives via email.

If offered a discount, coupon or freebie on the spot in exchange for their email address, some consumers will give you false email addresses to get the reward. To protect your list quality, deliver any signup incentives to the email address provided. That encourages people to give you their real address, as well as to make sure that they spelled or entered it correctly.

List Building

28

Set expectations regarding how many emails you'll be sending subscribers and what content will be in them.

The top two reasons given by subscribers for why they unsubscribe are consistently that they "received too many emails" and that "the emails weren't relevant." Use your signup messaging, signup confirmation page and welcome emails to set expectations appropriately. Consider providing images of or links to previous emails as examples of the kind of content you will send.

List Building

29

Keep your email signup forms short and simple, and collect additional information after signups.

For most brands, the only piece of information that is absolutely necessary for an email signup is the person's email address. Every bit of information beyond that adds friction to the process and decreases signups.

There are many opportunities to collect additional information after an email signup, including your opt-in confirmation page, preference center, welcome emails, registration forms, online checkouts, and progressive profiling efforts such as email surveys. As a relationship grows, subscribers will be willing to share progressively more information.

If you do require more information at signup for business or compliance reasons, consider breaking the signup process into two or more steps, where each step consists of a short form.

List Building

30

Recognize that requiring email subscribers to share additional contact information lowers signups significantly.

Consumers are fairly willing to share their email addresses with brands, which is one of the attractive traits of email marketing. But people are significantly more guarded when it comes to sharing their mailing address, phone number and cellphone number—especially if they think it will expose them to additional marketing communications.

List Building

31

Only ask for information
you will use.

Whether on your subscription form, on your opt-in confirmation page, in your welcome email or further along in the email relationship, asking for information sets the expectation that you'll use it for the subscriber's benefit. Don't ask for information that you think you might use eventually. You can always get that information later and in the meantime you won't be setting false expectations or dampening the response to a form.

For instance, don't ask subscribers which product categories they are most interested in if you don't plan on using that information to create targeted messages.

List Building

32

Explain to subscribers how sharing additional information with you will benefit them.

If you require additional information, tell subscribers how you will use it to their benefit. For instance, if you require their zip code so you can send them news about local events or merchandise only carried by stores near them, make that clear. If you require their birth date (perhaps for regulatory reasons) and will use it to send them a special birthday offer, tell them that and make sure you're prepared to follow through.

List Building

33

Ask the right questions when profiling subscribers.

Try to be as direct as possible when asking about interests and collecting other information during signups, in your preference center or elsewhere. Avoid making assumptions.

For instance, if you want to know if a subscriber is interested in men's or women's apparel, ask them that. Don't ask their gender and assume that men are only interested in buying clothes for themselves.

Similarly, if you have brick-and-mortar stores, don't ask for a subscriber's zip code and assume that their preferred store is the one that's closest to their home. It may be your store that's closest to their workplace or elsewhere, so use their zip code as a starting point but give them the freedom to select a different location.

List Building

34

Use the signup confirmation page
to continue to engage
new subscribers.

When a person signs up to receive your emails, they are reaching out to you and expressing a desire to hear more from you. So don't stop talking after they subscribe.

In addition to clearly confirming that the person just signed up to receive promotional emails from you, the opt-in confirmation page can be used for any number of purposes that capitalize on the moment and engage the new subscriber further.

For instance, it could be used to ask subscribers to add your email address to their address book, to collect optional preferences and other information, to drive them to key webpages, to educate them about sister brands or to expose them to your social media channels.

If you plan on sending a welcome email immediately, you can tell the subscriber to look for that. And if you know that some of your emails are being routed to "junk" or "spam" folders, you can use the signup confirmation page to ask them to check there if they don't see the welcome email in their inbox.

While it could be used in all those ways, it's best to focus on one or two of them, as asking subscribers to do too many things at once often lowers response.

List Building

35

Keep your signup process and preference center up to date and routinely audit all your acquisition sources to make sure they are working properly.

Keeping an inventory of all your acquisition sources and tracking their performance is the first step toward identifying problems that might arise from technology and process changes. But regularly checking these subscription pathways for errors is also advised.

You should also routinely eyeball your signup language and preference center content. For example, make sure you're not offering choices that you can no longer honor, such as a discontinued newsletter or content choice. Also, if you're asking about equipment, items or brands your subscribers own, make sure those selections are up to date.

Welcome Emails

In addition to confirming a successful signup, welcome emails reach new subscribers when they are most engaged. These are among the most effective emails you can send and are key to getting the email relationship off to a good start.

WORDS TO KNOW

---

welcome email
A message automatically sent to a new subscriber just after they've opted in that welcomes them to your email program and seeks further engagement

welcome email series
Multiple emails automatically sent to a new subscriber over time that seek to maximize engagement

---

Welcome Emails

36

Send a welcome email immediately after signup.

Consumers have been trained to look to their inbox after subscribing, registering and checking out, so the longer you wait before sending a welcome email the more likely the subscriber will move on to other things. Sending a welcome email immediately maximizes its effectiveness by continuing the momentum of a signup and engaging the subscriber further.

Welcome Emails

37

Send a series of welcome emails to warm up subscribers.

While sending even one welcome email prevents subscribers from abruptly being dropped into your promotional email stream, most brands can ease that transition further and engage subscribers more quickly and more deeply by sending multiple introductory emails.

For instance, you might want to send a new subscriber (1) a rich welcome offer to try to get that first conversion, followed by (2) an email explaining your brand's strengths, such as your standing free shipping offer, exclusive products and generous return policy, followed by (3) an email discussing the benefits of downloading your mobile app or engaging with you on social media, and concluding with (4) an email reminding them that their welcome offer is expiring in a few days, if they haven't taken advantage of that offer already.

Welcome Emails

38

Message new subscribers differently depending on their acquisition source.

Consumers who opt into your email program during checkout online or in one of your stores are likely much more familiar with your brand and products than people who opt in through your homepage—particularly if you sell expensive products like motorcycles or cruise vacations. Treat these people differently by sending them different content in your welcome emails.

Similarly, if a person signs up for email on your Facebook page, then you probably shouldn't be pushing them to "like" you in your welcome emails. Instead, use that opportunity to promote something they're more likely to be unfamiliar with such as your mobile app.

Welcome Emails

39

Include an unsubscribe link
in your welcome emails.

Well-crafted welcome emails are promotional emails, so even though a subscriber just extended permission to you to send them email, they have a legal right to immediately take that permission back upon receiving your welcome email.

Poorly crafted welcome emails that simply confirm the signup and nothing more might technically qualify as transactional emails and not be legally required to have an unsubscribe link under CAN-SPAM. However, regardless of whether you take advantage of the promotional power of welcome emails, it's wise to view them as promotional emails in spirit since the subscriber has just asked you to send them promotional emails and this is the first email you're sending them.

And in the same way that you can use a confirmed opt-in process to protect your list from low-quality acquisition sources, you can use a more prominent unsubscribe link in your welcome email to give regretful subscribers a clear way to opt-out rather than mark your email as spam. A prominent opt-out link can also build trust by signaling to subscribers that you'll make it easy for them to unsubscribe in the future as well. Prominent opt-out links are typically positioned in the upper right-corner of the email design opposite your logo, in addition to the usual position at the bottom of the email in the footer.

Welcome Emails

40

Pay special attention to subscribers during their first few weeks on your list, as this is when they are likely to be most responsive.

This "honeymoon" period of heightened engagement right after signing up is one of the reasons that a strong series of welcome emails is so important, but you may find that other actions are also worth taking. For instance, if a subscriber signed up for a weekly or monthly email program and your next regular email isn't due for a while, send the most recent email immediately to start demonstrating the value of your program.

Email Content & Design

Whether it's catalogs, billboards, TV ads or email, every channel has their own unique best practices for creating messages that make the most of the channel.

Email is unique in a few ways. First, there are at least two stages to interacting with a message: viewing the envelope content, then viewing the body content, which usually also involves scrolling. Second, email is read on a variety of devices in a variety of places. And third, most email messages ask and enable subscribers to take immediate action.

WORDS TO KNOW

---

envelope content
The portion of an email that's visible to subscribers before they open it

sender name
The name that appears in the "From" line in an email reader

subject line
The text that appears in the "Subject" line in an email reader

body content or copy
The text, images and other content inside your email that becomes visible when opened

preheader text
HTML text positioned at the very top of an email that is most often used to reinforce or extend the subject line

snippet text
A portion of the first text from inside the email that some email readers display after the subject line in the inbox, when highlighting a new email's arrival, or in other situations

---

Email Content & Design

41

Use a recognizable and consistent sender name.

While much is written about the power of a good subject line, the identity of the email sender has a greater impact on whether the recipient opens it. The sender name, which appears as the "From" name on emails, is the first thing that many email users look at when receiving an email and many ignore, delete or mark as spam any emails from senders they don't instantly recognize.

For this reason, it's critical to use a sender name that subscribers will immediately recognize. For most marketers, that will be your brand name.

Avoid using generic terms such as "newsletter," "info" and "customer service," as well as parent company names, as consumers are not always aware of the relationship between companies. And avoid using the name of your CEO, president or other officers, as people are not always aware of who your leaders are. Also, leaders come and go, but your brand name is far less likely to change.

Once you decide on the appropriate sender name to use, always use that name so subscribers are trained to look for it. Don't change it for "special" one-off emails. Having an email come "from" a person's name doesn't make it more authentic or sincere; it just makes it more difficult for recipients to recognize your emails. Instead, use the subject line to indicate that the email is a message from a particular person.

Email Content & Design

42

Keep your subject lines short but still coherent.

People are in a hurry as they scan their inboxes and decide which emails to open. Overly long subject lines are a turnoff to many consumers and don't lead to more clicks or conversions among those who do open.

At the other end of the spectrum, very short subject lines often generate higher-than-average open rates, but lower-than-average click rates. These subject lines tend to be more intriguing and mysterious, but as a result attract curious subscribers rather than the subscribers who are most likely to answer the calls-to-action in the email. Plus, using too many vague, short subject lines may cause fewer subscribers to open your emails over time because the email content has repeatedly disappointed them.

While growing smartphone readership will continue to put downward pressure on subject line length, the sweet spot appears to be in the neighborhood of 20 to 40 characters, which generally produces above average conversions and clicks, as well as opens. That tends to be enough characters to clearly convey two or more attributes of the email's content, including the topic, value, urgency and relevance to the subscriber, while staying true to your brand's voice.

Be aware that word choice can affect perceived subject line length, since several long words can be easier to read than a bunch of short words.

Of all the topics covered in this book, subject lines are the most frequently tested—and rightfully so. The perfect subject line lies at the intersection of your intended message, your unique brand, and your unique set of subscribers. Finding that point requires a deep understanding of all three elements, a process that's as much art as it is science.

Email Content & Design

43

Recognize that even if an email is not opened, the sender name still delivers a brand impression and a subject line can deliver a call-to-action.

While every marketer wants every single one of their emails opened, very few subscribers are that engaged. Even so, emails still generate value when they go unopened by subscribers who at least occasionally engage with your emails.

First, a subscriber who deletes an email unopened is still exposed to your brand name in the "from" line, which helps keep your brand top of mind and might prompt interactions in other channels.

Second, if the subject line is clear about what action you want subscribers to take, it has an even better chance of prompting interactions in other channels or generating word of mouth. For instance, a subject line about summer apparel might serve as a general reminder for the subscriber to stop by their local store to refresh their summer wardrobe. And including a promo code in a subject line might spur a subscriber to make a purchase without even needing to open the email.

And third, the subject line can affect subscriber interest in opening future emails. For example, if the subject line promotes a good deal but the recipient is just not in the market to shop at the moment, the savings message still reaffirms the subscriber's belief in the value of your emails and would keep them interested in future emails.

For those reasons, avoid relying too much on vague and mysterious subject lines to generate opens. Over time this can erode trust by making subscribers feel misled by your subject lines and forced to open your emails to find out what they're about.

Instead, try to be descriptive, using keywords connected to the primary message and maybe an important secondary message. A subject line should help subscribers decide whether opening the email will be a good use of their time. And respecting your subscribers' time makes them less likely to tune you out and more likely to stay subscribed.

Email Content & Design

44

Measure the success of a subject line by how well it drives clicks and conversions.

Just because subscribers sequentially interact with your subject line, your email and finally your website content before converting, don't be tempted to believe that subject lines only affect opens.

A good subject line is one that predisposes subscribers who open to be receptive to the content of the email and ultimately convert at a higher rate. Put another way, a good subject line preselects openers so that those subscribers who open an email are the ones mostly likely to be interested in its contents. So a subject line that produces fewer opens but more conversions is preferable to one that produces more opens but fewer conversions.

When evaluating subject lines, also be sure to look at unsubscribe and spam complaints rates, as you always want to keep these rates low.

Email Content & Design

45

Support your subject line with preheader text.

Preheader text plays a unique role in email design because while it's technically body copy, it's also sometimes envelope copy. That's because some email readers display some of the first text from inside the email after the subject line in the inbox when highlighting a new email's arrival or in other situations. When that happens, the portion of preheader displayed as envelope copy is called snippet text.

You can make the most of snippet text by making sure that your preheader text supports or extends the subject line of your email. Avoid having your preheader repeat the subject line.

Preheaders may also include links to view the web-hosted version of the email, to visit your social media pages, to update preferences and to unsubscribe. If you include any of those options in your preheader, don't make them the first text in your emails as that squanders the opportunity provided by snippet text.

Similarly, don't ask your subscribers to add your email address to their address book or Safe Sender list in the preheader of every email you send. Make that request on your signup confirmation page and in your welcome email series. If subscribers haven't done it after being asked a few times, they're unlikely to ever do it and you're just wasting valuable screen real estate by endlessly asking.

Also, the importance of preheader text is growing along with smartphone readership because preheader text occupies a more prominent position on small screens. Be sure to link all or a portion of your preheader text so subscribers can immediately click through and take action.

WORDS TO KNOW

---

email template
Preformatted email file that includes all the elements you want to appear in every email, plus spots for content that changes from email to email

rendering
How an email reader translates an email's coding and displays the email

image blocking
When ISPs or subscribers stop the images in an email from loading

defensive design
Design techniques that allow an email to communicate its message effectively when images are blocked

alt *text*
Text coded into an <img> tag that is displayed when the image is blocked and when recipients mouse over the image, although support is not consistent

HTML or system text
Text from a limited number of fonts that are universally or widely supported across email readers

graphical text
Text that is part of an image

anatomy of an email

Below is a diagram of a basic email design, containing the most common elements. Many permutations are possible, especially within the grey portion of the diagram, which is where images tend to be used

preheader

header
navigation bar
primary message
secondary message
social media bar

footer

header
The portion of an email that includes your brand's logo

navigation bar
A row of links to important pages on your website

primary message or content block, or hero
The main message of an email, which is usually positioned at the top of the email and larger than other messages in the email

secondary message or content block
The other message(s) in an email, usually following and smaller than the primary message

product grid
A multi-column and usually multi-row layout where each grid cell contains a product image and other information such as product name, brand and price

---

Email Content & Design

46

**Use a single, flexible
email template for all your
routine promotional emails.**

Creating lots of email templates invites errors and
multiplies the effort it takes to maintain and
optimize them. While you'll want to use different
templates for your transactional and other
triggered emails (which we'll discuss later), create
a single template for your routine promotional
emails that allows you to swap out elements in
order to make any email message you need.

Email Content & Design

47

Design your emails to render well and function across a wide range of platforms and devices.

Very few subscribers will open your emails more than once, so it's critical that your emails display well on smartphones, desktops and everything in between.

Support for HTML and CSS coding varies across email readers and browsers, and support can change without notice, so it is important to use a rendering preview tool or routinely view your emails in a wide range of email readers to check for inconsistencies.

This issue has become more critical as more subscribers read email on their smartphones, where small screens can make it difficult to easily read and engage with promotional emails that are not designed with mobile devices in mind. You can no longer expect subscribers who have a lackluster experience with a promotional email on a mobile device to save those emails and reopen them later on a laptop or desktop. The vast, vast majority will just hit "delete."

The growing use of smartphones to read emails also opens up new email design opportunities. For instance, make any phone numbers in your emails tappable so subscribers can instantly make that call.

Email Content & Design

48

Design each of your emails so they convey their message even when images are blocked.

Many email readers block images by default and some subscribers don't turn images on, so relying too heavily on images to communicate your message can be a losing strategy. Defend against image-blocking ruining your message by using two common "defensive design" techniques: adding *alt* text to your image coding, and using HTML or system text as much as feasible instead of embedding text in your images.

The *alt* text of an image generally appears when the image is blocked and when recipients mouse over the image, although support isn't consistent. If an image contains graphical text, use the *alt* text to replicate all or some of that text so recipients can read it when images are not enabled.

HTML text is limited to just a small number of popular font families—including Ariel, Courier New and Times New Roman—but these fonts are universally supported. And in most cases, the fonts can also be styled in different sizes, colors and type treatments (bold, etc.).

Use HTML text at the very top of your emails

before the header to create preheader text, which most often communicates the primary call-to-action of the email or builds on the content of the subject line. It can also be used for your navigation bar links; throughout your primary and secondary messaging blocks, particularly for headlines, coupon codes and calls-to-action; and in a product grid. And, of course, HTML text should be used for all footer text and administrative links, such as your mailing address and unsubscribe link.

Using these defensive design tactics is especially critical in the first emails that a consumer receives from you, such as welcome and transactional emails.

WORDS TO KNOW

---

call-to-action (CTA)
What a message asks a subscriber to do, but more specifically the buttons and links subscribers click to take action

above the fold
The portion of an email that's displayed before a subscriber scrolls

below the fold
The portion of an email that's only displayed after a subscriber scrolls

share with your network (SWYN)
Functionality that allows subscribers to add content from your email to their social media timeline so their friends can see it

forward to a friend (FTAF)
Providing a link in your email that takes subscribers to a form that allows them to forward all or a portion of your email or a particular message promoted in your email to one or more of their friends

---

Email Content & Design

49

Design your emails so
they can be easily scanned.

Subscriber don't read emails; they scan them. So make it easy for subscribers to scan your email content by creating a clear hierarchy of content and calls-to-action (CTAs).

Use strong headlines that are substantially larger than the text that falls under them. The primary message block, or hero, should be larger than any secondary content blocks and should immediately, or at least closely, follow the header and navigation bar. And the key CTAs should be large and ideally in the form of buttons so they stand out.

Using phrases and bulleted items rather than full sentences also makes email content easy to scan. If you have to use full sentences, avoid blocks of text that are more than five lines long as large blocks of text discourage readers.

In most cases your email is just a gateway to your website or some other final destination, so you don't need to include every detail of an offer. You just need to convey the highlights in a way that compels subscribers to click through, and they can bet the rest of the details then.

Email Content & Design

50

Design your email content in screen-sized chunks.

Don't design your emails like posters or store signage. Unless a particular email is small, subscribers don't see an entire email at once, but rather in screen-sized chunks as they scroll through it. While how much of an email is displayed at one time varies by device and email reader, a good rule of thumb is to design your emails assuming that subscribers will only be able to see about 300 pixels of height at a time.

That doesn't mean that all your content has to be limited to small chunks, but it does mean that larger blocks of content should make sense when viewed a little at a time.

Email Content & Design

51

Pay extra attention to the top portion of your email that appears "above the fold" and make sure it is well branded.

The email content that appears "above the fold" on that first screen-sized chunk is the most critical. That's because some subscribers will not scroll down to see the content that's "below the fold." Again, it's helpful to assume that your subscribers will only be able to see 300-pixel-tall chunks of your email at a time on average.

The standard promotional email begins with preheader text. That's followed by the header, which includes your brand's logo. That's followed by a navigation bar that provides links to key pages on your website, and then the primary content block that includes your main message.

Having your logo visible above the fold is essential as it provides additional confirmation of who the sender is. Most marketers position their logo on the left-hand side of the header, so it's seen immediately as subscribers scan downward from the left-hand side of the screen. However, it's not uncommon for logos to be centered.

Avoid having multiple lines of preheader text or an overly large logo as these push your primary message further down in the email so that less of it appears above the fold.

Similar to the navigation bar on your website, email nav bars can serve as a significant source of clicks by offering a quick path to important pages on your website.

Just because the top portion of your email is the most read, don't try to cram lots of content up top. Content still needs room to breathe. But you'll probably want to position headlines and other key text toward the top of your primary content block so at least part of it appears above the fold.

Email Content & Design

52

Don't design your email to mirror your website's design exactly.

You should use consistent branding and general style across all your channels, including email. At the same time, recognize that every channel is different.

For example, emails enjoy less design freedom than websites because of inferior and inconsistent coding support across all the various email readers available. Emails have less screen real estate to work with than websites because emails share the screen with inbox navigation as well as ads, in many cases. And subscribers often act differently than website visitors because they are more engaged with your brand and because emails aren't usually intended to deliver a complete experience without clicking through to a website.

So don't shrink your website design down and use it in your emails. Instead, design your emails so they incorporate key branding elements from your website while being optimized for the email channel. Use the same color scheme, but be flexible on the layout and design elements such as fonts, opting for a widely supported HTML font rather than the exact font you use on your website, for instance.

Navigation bars are another area where you're better off using a derivative of what's on your website. Because emails are generally narrower than websites, you typically only have room for three to six links, depending on whether your nav bar sits to the right of your logo or under it, so think about the nav links that will be of most interest to your email subscribers. Also consider changing up your nav bar links from one email to the next in order to support the primary message of each one.

Email Content & Design

53

Create an email content calendar.

Many large marketers start working on an email weeks or even months before the send date—and start planning their holiday email promotions as early as July. Having an email content calendar allows you to not only secure ample time to plan and execute an email, but also to make sure you have a good mix of email content and are focused on key selling periods during the year.

Having a content calendar also lets you plan for occasions when you need to have multiple content options available to respond to potential outcomes, such as promoting gear from the winner of the Super Bowl, albums of Grammy winners, or products pegged to whether the groundhog saw his shadow or not.

You can't plan for everything, however. Sometimes news and other events provide great marketing opportunities. Give yourself the flexibility to leverage those to promote your products and serve your customers.

Email Content & Design

54

Provide context for products featured in your emails.

Don't assume that subscribers know what your products are for, how to use them, or the differences between similar products. It's important for you to provide context for your products to help inspire subscribers to buy, as well as to remove barriers to buying.

For instance, an apparel retailer might show the same blouse used in two outfits, one dressed up and one dressed down, to show its versatility. An electronics retailer might link to an article or blog post that explains the different kinds of HDTV display technologies. And a home improvement retailer might promote a video that demonstrates all the uses of a power washer.

All brands should think of themselves as publishers.

Email Content & Design

55

Give your customers and other people a voice in your emails.

Consumers trust what others do and say more than they trust what companies say, so give your customers, outside experts, media outlets, bloggers, celebrities and others a presence in your emails.

Consider promoting top-selling, top-rated, most-liked, most-tweeted and most-pinned items, and including pictures, video, testimonials, reviews, tweets, and other content provided by customers. Poll your customers and include the results in an email.

Also consider including advice, curated product assortments and other content from outside experts, as well as pointing out media coverage of your products. The voice of your staffers can also ring more true than anonymous, disembodied corporate content.

Email Content & Design

56

Offer subscribers non-promotional calls-to-action and content.

While the goal of your email program is likely to generate sales, that doesn't mean that every message has to scream "Buy Now."

Subscribers are not always in the market to buy your products, so incessantly asking them to buy can be off-putting and cause them to tune you out. Non-promotional content breaks up the constant hard sell but can also inspire and motivate subscribers to buy when they didn't consider themselves in the market. Even emails that have a completely non-promotional primary message and no secondary messages are effectively promotional, too, so long as they have a header and navigation bar that links to your website.

For all those reasons, balance your promotional content with some educational, instructional, editorial and inspirational content. This could take the form of surveys and polls that give you progressive profiling data, updates on social media activity, information about your charity or conservation efforts, or season's greetings and other messages of thanks.

Email Content & Design

57

Use faster channels to help determine the content of your emails.

Improve the results of your email marketing campaigns by incorporating learnings from faster channels like site search, pay-per-click (PPC) search campaigns and Twitter.

For instance, look at the terms that visitors are putting into your website's search box and use popular terms in your subject lines or body copy. You can also fine tune the landing page of a PPC search campaign before using it for an email campaign or use insights from PPC search ad headlines and body copy for subject lines and preheader text.

Similarly, you can use the results of your email campaigns to inform slower channels like catalogs.

Email Content & Design

58

Make your calls-to-action clear in language and positioning.

If you want subscribers to do something, tell them by using direct language in your calls-to-action (CTAs). If you want them to buy a product, use a "Buy Now" CTA rather than a generic "click here" CTA.

Similarly, place your CTAs so that they punctuate the copy that's associated with it. For example, if you want subscribers to share a discount code in an email with their friends and family on Twitter, Facebook and other social networks, place a share-with-your-network (SWYN) link with a "Share this deal" CTA right next to the discount code just as you'd place a "Buy Now" button next to product information.

Email Content & Design

59

Offer many paths to click through.

When we talk about calls-to-action, we're generally referring to buttons and text links. But subscribers have a much broader definition of a CTA. They see the logo in your header, headlines and pretty much any image in your email, whether it is a product shot or not, as a CTA that they'll try to click. Make the most of their interest by making as many of these elements clickable as possible.

That said, don't cluster non-identical links too closely together as subscribers reading your email on tablets and, in particular, smartphones may have difficulty accurately selecting a link with their finger.

Email Content & Design

60

Don't limit your calls-to-action to online only.

Email can drive subscribers to act offline just as effectively as it can drive them to act online, so don't shy away from promoting store events and other happenings. In fact, the increase in emails being read on smartphones is making offline calls-to-actions more effective because subscribers can increasingly be reached when they are out and about.

Subscribers are more likely to be out of the home on weekends, during the warmer months, and especially on big shopping days like Thanksgiving Day, Black Friday and the day after Christmas. Those are all occasions to be more mindful of mobile readers and to include store-only deals, mobile coupons, and store-specific information such as hours in your emails.

WORDS TO KNOW

---

weight
The file size of the HTML coding of an email

animated gif
An image file that displays multiple images over time

live content
Images and other email content that vary based on when the email is opened, what kind of device it's opened on, and other factors

recovery module
A multi-column secondary content block, usually positioned right before the footer, that contains many links to different product categories, brands or other areas of your website that is designed to appeal to subscribers who were uninterested in the other calls-to-action in the email

social media bar
A row of social media icons that link to your brand's pages on those social media sites

footer
The text at the bottom of an email that includes the promotional fine print, legal language, unsubscribe link, mailing address and other details

---

Email Content & Design

61

Keep the weight of your emails reasonable.

When the file size of an email message is too large, ISPs may only display part of your message or block it altogether. Very large emails also load more slowly for subscribers, especially if they use mobile devices, which may cause them to hit "delete" in frustration.

As network and device speeds change in the years ahead, guidelines and limits on email file sizes will change too. But for now, it's best to keep the HTML coding of your emails to 60 KB or less, and definitely don't exceed 100 KB.

Note that this doesn't include the file size of web-hosted images associated with an email, which could be an additional several hundred kilobytes—or even more for graphically heavy messages.

Email Content & Design

62

Do not include attachments
on your emails.

Consumers are very hesitant to open attachments because of the risk of viruses and other malicious payloads. For that same reason, plus the fact that attachments often dramatically increase the weight of your email, ISPs and corporate email servers are more likely to block your emails if you include attachments.

Instead, host any PDF coupons, documents or other files on the web and link to them from the email or, even better, link to a webpage that lets subscribers download these materials and then easily navigate to other parts of your website.

Email Content & Design

63

Use motion selectively to engage subscribers.

Since most email content is static, movement really stands out in an email.

Animated gifs are the most common mechanism for adding motion to email because most email readers support them. Animation can be used to demonstrate how a product works, show color or style variations of a product, draw attention to a call-to-action or secondary message, or add some fun and whimsy to a design.

Small animations can be just as effective as large ones, and too many animations in an email can feel overly busy and distract from your message. Be mindful of the size and number of frames in your animated gifs to prevent the file size from getting too large.

Some email readers block animated gifs and only show the first frame of the animation. You may want to plan for that possibility by using an image that can stand on its own as your first frame. Sometimes that means placing the last frame of your animation first.

You can also use video content, live content and other mechanisms to add motion to your email designs, but be aware that support for these is inconsistent across email readers.

Email Content & Design

64

Don't include sound effects or auto-play videos with sound enabled by default in your emails.

People expect the internet to be a largely silent experience unless they press a "Play" button. That's even truer of their expectations around email, especially as more emails are read on mobile devices—in stores and restaurants, in meetings, during presentations and at other times when sounds might be unwelcome.

HTML5 video and other tools are making it easier to add playable video content to emails. Avoid the temptation to use sound as a tactic to stand out from the crowd.

Email Content & Design

65

Don't avoid long emails because you think subscribers won't scroll.

While higher email frequencies and more consumers reading emails on smartphones are driving many marketers to send shorter emails, subscribers will still engage with longer emails. Beyond having compelling content, marketers can use several techniques to encourage subscribers to scroll and in doing so expose them to more of the content in your emails.

First, use a single-column format as it makes it much easier for subscribers to scroll and scan your content than a two-column format does. Including product grids doesn't impede scrolling, but limit them to four columns wide or less.

Second, look for opportunities to use an S-curve layout, where an image on the left and text on the right is followed by an image on the right and text on the left, and so on. Subscribers often find this arrangement easier to read than having all images on the left and all text on the right, or vice versa.

Third, use images with strong vertical or sloping lines, as subscribers' eyes naturally follow these lines, especially if the image is only partially revealed. For instance, if subscribers see the top of a Christmas tree or part of a necklace chain, many will be intrigued enough to scroll to see the whole tree and entire necklace.

And fourth, consistently place some high-value content deep in your emails. If you stick with a consistent layout, subscribers will be trained to look for certain types of content throughout your email. For instance, if you always place a coupon at the bottom of your email—and perhaps even call attention to it with a short message in your header or in a small banner right below your header—subscribers will learn that they have to scroll down to find that coupon.

When you send long emails, be thoughtful about the content you place at the very bottom before the footer, as that content tends to attract more attention than the content that falls in the middle.

Email Content & Design

66

Don't expect subscribers to scroll back up to the top of your email.

While it's not unreasonable to expect subscribers to scroll to the bottom of even very long emails, it is unreasonable to expect them to scroll back up. For that reason, consider using content with a high link density at the bottom of your emails to give subscribers many alternatives to the message blocks higher up.

One tactic is to include a recovery module, which is a multi-column content block that contains many links to different product categories, product sub-categories, price points, or brands, for instance. Sometimes recovery modules are related to the theme of the email, but other times they just promote sale or clearance items in various product categories.

Another tactic is to repeat your navigation bar before your footer or elsewhere in the email.

Email Content & Design

67

Include links to
your social media pages.

Email subscribers are among your best customers and you can make them even better customers if you can also engage them through social media. Providing links to pages on Facebook, Twitter and elsewhere in your emails is a constant reminder that there are other ways to interact with your brand—and, more importantly, to see what other customers are saying.

Most marketers include these links right before their footer in a social media bar, but some include them in their header to the right of their logo. "Above the fold" space is precious, so if you include social community links in your header, make sure they are performing well enough to earn that position.

If you also include share-with-your-network (SWYN) links in your email template as well as social community links, consider differentiating them by prefacing your SWYN links with "Share:" and your social community links with "Follow Us:" or something similar.

Email Content & Design

68

Don't place anything important after your footer copy.

Subscribers have been trained to stop scrolling when they reach email footers, where you put all your offer exclusions and other legalese, administrative links like unsubscribe links, and mailing address for CAN-SPAM compliance. So anything positioned after your footer is likely to go unseen.

Email Content & Design

69

Use a consistent email design, but don't be afraid to occasionally deviate from it.

Having a consistent email design is brand-building, makes you more recognizable in the inbox and creates familiarity. However, it can also give the impression that all of your messages are equally important and can become monotonous to the point of lulling subscribers to sleep so that they pay less attention to you. Significantly changing your email design on a one-off basis every once in a while can deliver a "wake-up slap" that gets your subscribers' complete attention again.

Occasions where it might make sense to deviate from your usual email design include a major product launch, entry into a new product category, collaboration with another brand, a charity effort, a big social media or mobile campaign, or a win-back campaign aimed at reengaging subscribers who haven't clicked or converted in a long time.

In these situations, consider deviating from your email template in a significant way: depart from your usual color palette, use a shallow but wide creative where subscribers have to scroll to the right instead of down, drop your navigation bar and similar links to draw attention to your primary message, send a plain text email to express urgency, or "break the grid," where a portion of an image extends past the usual boundaries of the email.

While some consider these tactics "breaking the rules," I consider it a rule to periodically mix things up to keep things interesting and to create emphasis.

Email Content & Design

70

Keep a "swipe file" of your most successful email campaigns and components.

A swipe file is a record of your subject lines, emails and landing pages that performed really well. It's a file to return to for learnings and inspiration.

For instance, a swipe file helps you keep track of subject line arrangements, keywords and offers that your subscribers responded to best. It works the same for email designs, allowing you to model new designs off previously successful ones. You can even reuse past winners, although it's best to try to re-imagine, re-skin or further optimize them.

It's also wise to monitor what your competitors and others are doing with their email programs to get new ideas.

Seasonality

Consumers behave differently when they're buying for people other than themselves, and that's especially truly during November and December in the run up to Christmas. You should adapt the appearance, content and frequency of your emails to match those changes.

WORDS TO KNOW

---

seasonality
Related to an upcoming or current season, holiday or buying occasion

holiday header
A temporary header design that reflects seasonality

gift services footer
A secondary content block that is typically positioned just before the footer that pulls together links to order-by deadlines, gift guides, return policies and other important seasonal buying information

secondary navigation bar
A second nav bar that sits right under your standard nav bar that typically provides deeper navigation into one of your standard nav bar links, provides links to seasonal merchandise and content, or provides links that support the primary message or theme of the email

---

Seasonality

71

Alter your email design to highlight holidays and other seasonal events.

Just like stores hang garland, erect Christmas trees, and put up lots of red and green signage to indicate that the holiday season has arrived, email designs should also signal to subscribers that it's time to start thinking about gift-buying.

There are several ways to accomplish this. First, add seasonal imagery to your email designs, particularly your header since it appears above the fold.

Second, add a link to your navigation bar that directs subscribers to seasonal merchandise or your gift guide. You might also consider adding a holiday-themed secondary navigation bar dedicated entirely to promoting your seasonal merchandise and content.

And third, add a gift services footer, which pulls together links to order-by deadlines, gift guides, return policies and other important seasonal buying information into a single content block.

Seasonality

72

Make your emails and other email marketing pages seasonally relevant.

Just as your email design and content should respond to seasonality, other aspects of your email program can be similarly adjusted.

For instance, the email signup call-to-action on your homepage could be changed in November to say, "Don't miss our exclusive Black Friday email deals." You could also add a Valentine's Day gift services footer to your order confirmation emails in January and early February.

Seasonality

73

Send subscribers more email when they are in market or otherwise predisposed to take action.

Subscribers tolerate—and even welcome—more email when the email arrives at a time that's helpful to them.

For instance, retailers wisely send more promotional emails during the holiday season, knowing that their subscribers are actively looking for gift ideas and making many purchases. Similarly, many charities and other nonprofits send more email toward the end of the year, knowing that many people make most of their charitable donations just before the end of the calendar year for tax purposes.

As you increase email frequency during holiday periods, keep a close eye on how your subscribers respond. If engagement dips and spam complaints and unsubscribes rise too much, that's a sign to back down.

Seasonality

74

Message your subscribers differently during the holiday season.

Consumers use email differently during November and December than they do the other 10 months of the year. During the holiday season, people are extremely busy, travel more, may deal with bad weather, and have longer-than-usual lists of things to do in general. In short, they're more stressed.

They turn to promotional emails to make their lives easier by helping them find great gifts at great prices—and that's about it. Marketers can adjust their email content by simplifying, reducing or eliminating video and social media calls-to-action, contests, advice and lifestyle content, and other content that requires too much of a time commitment from subscribers. The holiday season is the time to simplify messaging.

It's also a time to increase customer service messaging, such as clarifying return policies, promoting order-by deadlines and highlighting store hours.

Seasonality

75

Recognize that once-a-year gift-buying makes subscribers' interests less predictable during the holiday season.

Consumers are mostly buying for others during the holiday season, so it's wise to downplay or disregard topic preferences and previous browse and purchase behavior. Promote a wider selection of products and product categories and direct subscribers to a gift guide that helps them find gifts by interest, gender, age, price or other variables. Also consider promoting fewer product category sales in favor of more sitewide sales.

Similarly, be wary of using the behavior of subscribers in December to send them tailored messages in January.

Targeting

While "one size fits all" broadcast emails will likely always comprise at least a slim majority of the messaging we send, their effectiveness is steadily declining. Consumers expect more. They expect marketers to listen to them—both to what they say and how they act—and respond with messages that are tailored to their interests.

This takes more effort than broadcast emails, but your subscribers will handsomely reward your efforts. Targeted emails often generate results that are multiple times better than those of broadcast emails, while simultaneously reducing unsubscribes and spam complaints.

With targeted messages on the rise, it's increasingly wise to think of your program's role less as email marketing and more as providing an email-powered personal shopper program that offers thoughtful recommendations, helpful advice and responsive customer service.

WORDS TO KNOW

---

targeting
Sending the right message to the right subscriber at the right time

expressed preferences
The topics, activities and other things that subscribers tell you they are interested in

implied preferences
The topics, activities and other things that subscribers indicate they are interested in based on their interactions with your brand

broadcast email
An email that is sent to all subscribers

segmentation
Sending a particular message to only those subscribers who are likely to respond based on their geography, demographics, behavior or other factors; or sending the same message to subscribers at different times based on their time zone or geography

dynamic content
A portion of a broadcast or segmented email that is tailored to different groups of subscribers based on their geography, demographics, behavior or other factors

personalization
Including information that's unique to the recipient in the subject line or body copy of an email

———————————

Targeting

76

Recognize that what subscribers do is more important than what they say.

Expressed preferences—that is, what subscribers tell you they are interested in or plan to do during signup, through progressive profiling and at other times—can become outdated rather quickly. People are not always the best judges of their own interests and sometimes their plans, intentions and circumstances change suddenly.

Expressed preferences are a good starting point, but are trumped by implied preferences communicated through subscriber behavior, especially as time passes. For example, if a subscriber says they are interested in hockey but begins buying baseball gear, then it would be wise to start mixing some baseball promotions into their emails.

As mentioned earlier, a major caveat to this is to be careful of giving much, if any, long-term weight to subscribers' browsing and purchase behavior during the holiday season.

Targeting

77

Send some segmented messages.

In addition to sending broadcast messages to your entire file, regularly use segmentation to send messages only those subscribers who are likely to respond. This makes your emails more relevant and increases your open, click and conversion rates, while reducing unsubscribes and spam complaints.

For instance, if you're opening a store, you should segment your list by zip code and only send a store opening announcement to your subscribers that live nearby. Segmenting by geography can also ensure that, for instance, all subscribers receive a promotion of winter gear at a time when their local temperatures start to get cool.

In addition to geography and demographics, you can also segment by subscriber interest, whether it's an interest they told you about explicitly or one that you've determined based on their browse behavior. For example, if you're promoting rock climbing gear, you could send the message only to those subscribers who have previously purchased that gear or who have browsed that product category in the past few months.

Targeting

78

Use dynamic content and personalization to add targeted content to emails.

Dynamic content and personalization are the tools that can make promotional emails a true form of one-to-one communication. They are like adding segmentation within an email message, with all of the same benefits. However, that segmentation can be ratcheted up so that it's at an individual level.

For instance, if you were promoting football jerseys in an email, you could use dynamic content to display images of players' jerseys from a subscriber's favorite team. You could also use body copy urge the subscriber by name to support their team. And you could take it up a notch further by personalizing an image of a team jersey with the subscriber's name.

Transactional emails such as order and shipping confirmation emails are full of personalization by definition, but there are opportunities to bring that same level of personalization into other kinds of emails.

Targeting

79

When personalizing content, have a good default set up for when you don't have data for a particular subscriber.

If you're personalizing an email, you can end up with some pretty embarrassing results when you try to pull a data point and encounter a null set. Protect yourself from blank spaces, showing code and other issues by establishing a default value for an attribute.

For example, if you're using first name personalization in a subject line, set a default value of "Valued Customer" or something jazzier like "Deal-Seeker" to avoid an awkward "Dear <$First_Name$>" in case you don't have a subscriber's name on record.

Targeting

80

Avoid misleading uses of personalization or suggesting that content is personalized when it is not.

Expectations are powerful. If you include a subscriber's name in a subject line, many subscribers will expect that the content in the email is tailored to them. If it's not, some of them will be disappointed. For that reason, it's best to reserve first name personalization in subject lines for emails that are segmented, contain dynamic content or personal information, or are sent directly in response to an action taken by a subscriber.

Similarly, in the body of an email, if you use language like "just for you" or "recommendations for you" and the content is generic, then you've trained your subscribers to pay less attention in the future when you use that language.

Targeting

81

Optimize the delivery time of your emails to increase their visibility in the inbox.

While ISPs and third-party tool providers have been increasingly offering features that threaten the "last in, on top" inbox paradigm, there's still an advantage to timing the arrival of your email so that it's at the top of the recipient's inbox or promotional email folder.

In general, the beginning of the work day (around 8 am), toward the end of the workday (around 4pm), and after dinner when the kids are in bed (around 8 pm) tend to be times when it's easiest to engage subscribers. Consider segmenting your list by time zone to target these periods more precisely.

However, as more and more emails are read on smartphones, these peak engagement periods are flattening out. Consider testing different send tactics for your mobile readers and desktop readers, or even trying to tailor send times to the behavior of individual subscribers.

You may also see a benefit in optimizing the day of the week that your emails are sent, although many brands find that decision is driven by promotions, store events and other factors out of their control. Targeting different days of the month, especially those around common paydays like the 15th and last day of the month, can also be fruitful.

WORDS TO KNOW

---

triggered email
A message that is sent to an individual subscriber in response to an action taken by that person or some event indicated by the subscriber

transactional email
Messages that are sent to an individual subscriber in response to that person making a transaction such as a purchase (i.e., order confirmation emails, shipping notification emails) or administrative request (i.e., password reset email, email address change confirmation email)

shopping cart abandonment email
Messages that are sent to an individual subscriber in response to that person leaving one or more items in their shopping cart

browse abandonment email
Messages that are sent to an individual subscriber in response to that person browsing certain pages of your website but not making a purchase

reengagement or win-back email
Messages that are sent to an individual subscriber in response to that person having not engaged with your emails or made a purchase in a long time in an effort to get them to engage and make a purchase again

---

Targeting

82

Include promotional and service content in your transactional emails.

An order confirmation email can and should do more than just confirm that a customer successfully placed an order. Transactional emails enjoy high open rates because they are expected and highly relevant to individual subscribers. Take advantage of that by including promotions and other content in your transactional emails that lead to more sales or improve customer satisfaction.

For example, if a customer buys a computer, you could promote accessories and software in the order confirmation email. Try to upsell buyers on accessories for the item they bought, on related or other affinity items, or on seasonal products.

That said, keep in mind that the main purpose of your transactional emails is to provide the customer with information about the transaction. To stay in compliance with CAN-SPAM's definition of a transactional email, it's wise to place additional content below the transactional content or in a right-hand column. It's also wise to limit the amount of promotional content to no more than about a quarter of the overall email.

Targeting

83

Create a variety of triggered emails to boost sales and improve customer service.

Triggered emails are among the highest performing emails you can send, regularly generating multifold more revenue per email than broadcast emails. They are super effective because they are delivered at a time when subscribers are most receptive to their content.

The key is to find events that can be used to trigger the right messaging. Common events and the messages they can trigger include:

- making a purchase >> order confirmation email, shipping confirmation email, delivery confirmation email, product review request email, short-supply and re-order emails, purchase anniversary email, service satisfaction survey email, other post-purchase emails

- registering at a site or for an event >> registration confirmation email

- leaving an item in a shopping cart >> shopping cart abandonment email

- requesting to be notified when an item is back in stock >> back-in-stock notification email

- browsing product pages without buying >>

browse abandonment email

- entering a contest or sweepstakes >> entry confirmation email, winner/loser notification email

- providing birth date of subscriber, spouse, children or pets, or date of wedding anniversary >> birthday email, wedding anniversary email

- signing up to receive email >> welcome email, signup anniversary email

- not engaging with promotional emails >> reengagement or win-back email, re-permission email

And you can surely think up many other instances where a triggered email would help, educate or reward your subscribers.

While some triggered emails perform best when sent immediately following the trigger, some perform better when sent on a delay. Some triggered messaging is more effective when done as a series of emails rather than a single one. And personalization can also greatly improve the effectiveness of some triggered emails.

Targeting

84

When using behavior for targeting, be careful not to come across like a stalker or Big Brother.

Subscriber behavior is wonderful for powering targeted messages, but some consumers are turned off by the idea that brands track their email and online activities. Be sensitive to these feelings by not acting on behavior triggers immediately and by not mentioning that you noticed their behavior.

For instance, if you have a browse abandonment email that's triggered by subscribers that browse cameras, you will probably want to wait a day or perhaps two before sending that email. And the email itself should just highlight great camera options and other helpful content without saying, "We noticed you looking at cameras..."

While some people will connect the dots, try to leave some doubt. Make it seem plausible that it's just a happy coincidence that the right content arrived at just the right time.

Targeting

85

Avoid offering special incentives in messages triggered by a non-purchase.

Subscribers catch on very quickly. If you reward bad behavior, they will behave badly.

For instance, if you send an incentive when they leave an item in their shopping cart, then they will abandon their carts every time and wait for the email incentive before purchasing. You will have trained your subscribers to delay their purchases and will have given margin away needlessly. It's now common behavior for many consumers to place items in their cart for consideration later—kind of like a wish list. So instead of offering an incentive, just email a reminder of the item(s) in their cart. That is often enough to spur many subscribers to go ahead and complete their purchase.

Save your triggered email incentives for when you really want to drive action, such as when you want to encourage a new subscriber to make their first purchase or win back a subscriber who hasn't made a purchase in a long time.

Targeting

86

Place a cap on triggered email volume and establish a messaging hierarchy.

Triggered messages are one of the best ways to deliver more email to your most engaged subscribers. However, even the most timely and relevant emails can become excessive if too many messages arrive too often.

To keep this from happening, place a cap on how many triggered emails a subscriber can receive over the course of a day, as well as a limit on how frequently a subscriber can receive the same triggered email.

For instance, if a subscriber browsed one product category and then another a few hours later, you probably shouldn't send them a browse abandonment email for each product category. You should pick one.

Also, you shouldn't send the same browse abandonment email again if the subscriber returns and browses the same product category again a week later.

In addition to caps, establish a message hierarchy to give priority to the most effective triggered emails. For instance, if a subscriber left an item in their shopping cart after browsing several items, you'd probably want to send a shopping cart abandonment email instead of a browse abandonment email.

Similarly, you might want to delay a product review request email if it was scheduled to go out on the same day as a birthday email to avoid having the two messages compete with each other.

Targeting

87

Keep an inventory of your triggered email programs and regularly schedule time to update and fine tune these.

Triggered emails are not "set it and forget it." As your brand strategy evolves, copywriting can be honed, design can be polished and targeting can be improved. Also take advantage of opportunities to add seasonal content to triggered emails to make them more relevant.

Besides making improvements, checkups are necessary to prevent errors. ISP support for coding changes over time, so neglected triggered emails can breakdown and not render properly. Promotions change, links become outdated, logos are updated—all are good reasons to keep a close eye on your triggered email programs.

Quarterly reviews are a good idea. Reviews are also wise any time your email template or website is significantly updated.

Inactivity

Sometimes subscribers aren't interested in your emails anymore but don't unsubscribe for some reason. Subscribers who haven't engaged with your emails in a long time represent a shrinking revenue opportunity and growing risk to your ability to get your emails delivered. They also dampen your performance metrics, making it more difficult to see positive changes. It's worth trying to get these subscribers engaged with your emails again, but realistically you'll end up letting most of them go.

WORDS TO KNOW

---

inactivity
When a subscriber has not opened or clicked in any of your emails in a long time

reactivate
Getting a subscriber to open or click one of your emails after a long period of having not done so

re-permission email
Messages that ask a subscriber to reconfirm their subscription by clicking on a link in the email in order to remain on your active mailing list

---

Inactivity

88

Define inactive subscribers by their email behavior, but consider their other behaviors.

ISPs don't care if a subscriber is one of your best customers. They only care if the subscriber is engaging with your emails by opening them, scrolling through them, clicking in them, forwarding them and taking other positive actions. And if they see that too many of your subscribers haven't engaged with your emails in a long time, they will take action and begin junking or blocking your emails.

However, you should care if emails reach your best customers, even if those customers don't appear to interact with those emails. As mentioned in Rule 13, measuring the interactions of your subscribers with your emails is not a perfect science, so you may want to delay actions when addressing inactives who you know to be good customers.

Inactivity

89

Send your inactive subscribers different messaging at a different frequency.

Once a subscriber has been inactive for many months, the chance of them becoming active again is small but definitely worth pursuing.

To try to reengage them, send inactive subscribers different emails than you send the rest of your list. Consider using different subject lines on your broadcast emails that go to actives and sending "win-back" emails with your richest offers. Also consider sending non-promotional content such as requests for them to update their email preferences or to complete a survey that might give you information you can use to send them targeted email.

Since ISPs use engagement metrics in their filtering algorithms, lots of inactive subscribers pose a risk to your deliverability. Reduce that risk by emailing inactives considerably less frequently. For instance, if you send daily emails, reduce that to weekly for inactives. Or if you send weekly emails, reduce that to once a month. In addition to protecting your deliverability, less frequent mailings can make some subscribers pay more attention to your emails.

Also, if you can identify subscribers who are at a high risk of becoming inactive, you can preemptively treat those subscribers differently as well in an effort to keep them active.

Inactivity

90

Send a series of re-permission emails before you remove a chronically inactive subscriber from your email list.

As explained in Rule 5, permission expires. But don't just remove a subscriber from your list without warning. Send a re-permission email that tells the subscriber that if they don't respond that they'll be removed from your email list. Essentially, you're asking them to re-confirm their subscription.

Send up to three re-permission emails. Use different subject lines and send them on different days and at different times of the day to increase response.

Response rates for re-permission emails tend to be very low, but they are worth the effort. Setting up an automated program to send these triggered emails takes relatively little work once you've set up a program to recognize and suppress chronically inactive subscribers.

Also, subscribers lost due to inaction may react positively to your courteous efforts if they discover the re-permission emails at a later date.

Landing Pages

Landing pages are the "last mile" of email marketing. Until subscribers are able to perform a transaction entirely within an email, landing pages will be vital to completing the conversation started by an email. If your emails generate good click rates, but your conversion rates are poor, your landing pages are likely to blame.

WORDS TO KNOW
_____

landing page
Webpage that subscribers are directed to when they click on a call-to-action in one of your emails
_____

Landing Pages

91

Design your landing pages so they look good and function well across a wide range of platforms and devices.

Just like emails must display well on a variety of email readers and devices, so too must landing pages. For instance, having a mobile-friendly email design is considerably less effective if subscribers have to click through to a website that's not optimized for mobile.

Landing Pages

92

Use language and images from the email on the landing page to create a smooth transition from email to landing page.

Give subscribers visual reassurances that they landed on the right page after clicking through an email by using some of the same language, images and other design elements. Doing so creates continuity between the email and the landing page that's comforting to subscribers. Subscribers who are unsure whether they've arrived at the right page may abandon your site or feel less certain about converting.

Landing Pages

93

Use a landing page that minimizes the number of clicks it takes for a subscriber to convert.

Every extra click you require a customer to make increases the chance that the customer will abandon your site, so take subscribers directly to the content they're expecting when they click through your email.

For example, if they click on a banner in your email that's promoting your clearance products, don't direct a subscriber to your homepage, even if there's a banner on your homepage promoting the clearance selection.

Too often, homepages are used as landing pages when a product category, product page, blog post or another page would save the subscriber a click or two.

Also consider the benefit of creating custom landing pages when there's no natural existing landing page for an email call-to-action.

Landing Pages

94

Don't make subscribers hunt for the items included in your emails.

If you use an item in an email to promote a product category, position that featured item prominently on the landing page. Don't make subscribers scroll through page after page of products to find the one you featured.

If you can't reposition the product on the landing page, consider providing a link to the item's product page in the email or including a caption in the email that includes the brand or name of the item so subscribers can at least search for it on your site.

And if you don't carry all the items in an image provided by the manufacturer, don't use the image. It erodes trust and frustrates subscribers when they can't find an item that you signaled you carried.

Landing Pages

95

Design well-branded landing pages and email administrative pages that offer a clear path forward.

Imagine you're walking through a store and see signs for a demonstration of a product you're interested in. You follow the signs to the back of the store and through a door that leads into the back alley, where you see the product demonstration going on. It's not the best brand impression, so chances are you're not going to stick around.

This same scenario plays out in email programs when subscribers are directed to barren pages with no branding and no navigation and no path forward. I call it "back alley syndrome" and it's most prevalent on pages that confirm an opt-out, preference update, signup, forward to a friend and other administrative functions. But it also occurs on email landing pages for videos, surveys and other special content that's used infrequently by a brand.

Dead-end pages prematurely end brand interactions and make bad impressions.

Landing Pages

96

Don't remove a landing page without providing an alternative landing page.

Products sell out and sales end, but if you remove email landing pages too quickly, subscribers can end up with "404 page not found" errors. That not only frustrates and confuses subscribers, who may not be sure if they've arrived at the right page or if a product is still available, but it fails to capitalize on their interest. Keep in mind that some subscribers will clickthrough an email days or even weeks after receiving it.

For product pages, if you plan on restocking the item, keep the page live. Consider offering visitors the option to sign up to receive a back-in-stock email notification when the item is available again. If the product is one-of-a-kind, consider redirecting visitors to similar items, preferable while notifying them that the item they originally sought has sold.

For sales event pages, consider redirecting visitors to a current sale page or posting a message that the sale has ended and suggesting other pages for them to visit.

Quality Assurance

It's easy to make mistakes in a medium that's high volume and lightning fast. In fact, it's inevitable. But in addition to regularly reviewing and updating your programs, there are steps you can take to minimize the chance of error.

WORDS TO KNOW

_____

quality assurance
Ensuring that email content is error-free and functions properly and that the intended subscribers receive that content at the intended time

apology email
Messages sent in response to an error or mishap

_____

Quality Assurance

97

Create a pre-send checklist.

The most common errors involve subject lines, typos, broken personalization and deployments. To reduce mistakes, use the following checklist as a starting point for your own:

☐ Do you have the right content scheduled for the right date? Double-check sends that are based on holidays whose dates change from year to year, such as Thanksgiving and Easter. And read the content one last time looking for errors.

☐ Do you have the right list? That's vital if you are segmenting the email, are running a test on a portion of your list, or operate multiple brands.

☐ Do you have the right personalization? Check the logic and assets for your personalization and dynamic content.

☐ Do you have the right sender name? It's particularly critical if you operate multiple brands.

☐ Do you have the right subject line? Avoid using placeholder text and don't leave subject line writing till the last moment.

☐ Do you have the right rendering? Use a rendering tool or view a test send in all the major email reader and browser combinations to make sure the message displays as intended.

☐ Do you have the right landing pages? Do all the links in the email lead to the correct pages, especially those for the key calls-to-action?

If content mistakes are routinely made, examine your production process and identify practices that invite errors or set up additional safeguards.

Quality Assurance

98

Take steps to reduce the impact of email marketing mistakes when they are discovered quickly.

When you discover a mistake with an email that you've just sent, there are a number of actions you can take to potentially fix the email post-send.

You have the best chance of fixing content errors. For instance, if the mistake is in an image, correct or replace the hosted source file for the image. If the mistake is with a link, see if you can get the link redirected to the correct page.

If the wrong list was used or if the error can't be fixed or fixed quickly, try to halt the send in order to reduce the number of subscribers that the incorrect email.

Also consider using social media and other channels to address any confusion caused by an email by emphasizing the correct information.

Quality Assuranc

info

99

Only resend emails or send apology emails for very serious errors.

Very few email errors rise to the level of needing to be corrected. Most errors are merely embarrassing, such as typos, or only affect a small portion of an email, such as broken links. Considering that most marketers now send more than one email a week and that any given email is only read by a small percentage of your subscribers, it's usually better just to move on.

However, if the error renders the email fairly nonfunctional and the email was promoting a major event or the email was unintentionally offensive and is causing significant brand damage, then action may be warranted.

It should be noted that most brands don't send a single apology email over the course of a year. And most of the apology emails that are sent are not in response to email errors, but rather site outages or other events.

For those rare instances when you do need to send an apology, it's wise to have a process in place so you can respond quickly. For instance, it's a good idea to have an apology email drafted that can be quickly updated with the necessary

Unsubscribe Process

Marketers tend to think of unsubscribes in very negative terms, but this negativity should be saved for spam complaints, which are a much more complete and utter form of failure. If a subscriber wants to leave your list, you'd much prefer they unsubscribe.

First and foremost, unsubscribes don't hurt your sender reputation, unlike spam complaints. Second, if someone unsubscribes, it indicates that they trust you to honor their opt-out, which is a positive sign from a brand perspective. And third, if they click the "unsubscribe" link, it gives you an opportunity to potentially address the reason that they're opting out or at least to honor their opt-out gracefully.

WORDS TO KNOW

opt-out process
How subscribers remove themselves from your mailing list

list churn
Subscribers lost to unsubscribes, spam complaints and bounces from email addresses that no longer work

unsubscribe page
Webpage that is launched when subscribers click the "unsubscribe" link in your emails and allows subscribers to complete the unsubscribe process

opt down

Allowing subscribers to choose to receive your emails less frequently

opt over

Giving subscribers the option to opt into one of your other channels, such as social or mobile, during your email unsubscribe process

---

Unsubscribe Process

100

List growth can also be boosted by reducing unsubscribes.

In order to grow your list on an absolute basis, your list growth has to exceed your list churn—that is, subscribers lost to unsubscribes, spam complaints and bounces from email addresses that no longer work. With most brands losing 25% or more of their subscribers each year, list churn is a significant drag on list growth. Developing strategies to reduce unsubscribes, as well as spam complaints, should be considered a part of list growth plans.

Unsubscribe Process

101

Clearly identify the subscriber on the opt-out page.

Give the subscriber assurances that they've arrived at their opt-out page or preference center by showing at least their email address prominently, if not other information such as their name. This helps prevent recipients of a forwarded email from unintentionally opting out a subscriber.

102

Give subscribers options in addition to completely opting out.

While you absolutely don't want to impede a subscriber from opting out, recognize that you might be able to address the issue that's driving a subscriber to unsubscribe.

A common reason for opting out is that the recipient felt they got "too many emails." Providing the ability to opt-down and receive fewer emails can retain the subscriber. "Once a month" and "once a week" are common opt-down email frequency choices.

Another common reason given is that "the emails were not relevant." Providing the subscriber the ability to select or change topic or product preferences can correct that problem.

Some subscribers simply want to change their email address and think they need to unsubscribe and resubscribe. Providing a "change your email address" option simplifies this process and eliminates the risk that they never get around to re-subscribing after opting out.

Others may still want to receive messages from you but would prefer to get them via another channel. You may be losing an email subscriber, but if you give them the ability to opt-over to direct mail, a social network or some other touchpoint then you'll keep the lines of communication open.

If you have sister brands, giving outgoing subscribers the option to sign up for emails from those brands may also pay off.

And lastly, when given the option to "stay subscribed," a surprising number of subscribers take that option, an indication that some are just exploring their options. Remind subscribers of the benefits of receiving your emails and give them the chance to re-affirm their subscription.

Unsubscribe Process

103

Be gracious as subscribers opt out.

Just because a subscriber doesn't want to receive any more emails from you doesn't necessarily mean that they don't ever intend to buy anything from you ever again. It also doesn't mean that they'll stop interacting with you via other channels. So be polite and gracious.

For instance, say that you're sorry to see them go and hope that they'll re-subscribe in the future. If you're a restaurant, thank them for being a subscriber and say that you hope to see them in one of your restaurants soon. If you're a nonprofit, reiterate the importance of your mission and that you appreciate their support.

Whatever you do, don't act like the relationship is over, because it most likely isn't. And even if the relationship is over for the moment, nothing is permanent.

Unsubscribe Process

104

Confirm unsubscribes via the channel through which they are requested.

Most unsubscribe requests come through your website when a subscriber clicks on the unsubscribe link in one of your emails. Confirm those opt-outs on your website. Sending an email confirming that a subscriber opted out may irritate them—perhaps to the point that they hit the "report spam" button.

The negative risks associated with these emails usually outweigh any benefits, such as helping protect against the rare cases of malicious opt-outs, when a person uses your opt-out page to unsubscribe someone else, or cases of recipients of a forwarded email unintentionally opting out a subscriber.

One exception to this is if the subscriber is paying to receive the emails or paying for a service that operates primarily through the emails. In that case, an opt-out confirmation email is really more of a termination of service notification.

Also, if you allow subscribers to opt-out by replying to one of your emails with "unsubscribe" or some other word in the subject line, then sending those people an opt-out confirmation email is completely appropriate.

Unsubscribe requests that come through your call center can be verbally confirmed on the spot. And requests that come through the mail should be confirmed in a letter as well.

Unsubscribe Process

105

Routinely audit your unsubscribe process to make sure it is working properly.

Consumers expect you to honor unsubscribe requests immediately and often report any additional emails they receive afterward as spam. But CAN-SPAM also requires that you honor unsubscribe requests swiftly, so this is not just a matter of quality assurance and good customer service, but of legal responsibility. If you use an email service provider to handle opt-outs through the unsubscribe link in your email, then you probably don't have to worry much about that opt-out path.

However, if you allow subscribers to opt-out by replying to your emails with "unsubscribe" or some other word in the subject line, by speaking with a call center representative, or by writing a letter, it's wise to check those processes periodically.

Testing

A vigorous testing program is the hallmark of a great email program. It is a critical form of listening and helps your program to be more user-friendly. Testing different subject lines, email designs, offers, content, and landing pages allows you to better understand your subscribers—what motivates them, what interests them and what appeals to them.

While uncovering huge performance differences is rare, keep in mind that small improvements add up to big results over time.

WORDS TO KNOW

A/B or split testing
Sending one version of an email to a portion of your subscribers and another slightly different version to another portion of your subscribers and seeing which version performed better, often with the winning version being sent to the remainder of your list

champion
Your existing design or process

challenger
The design or process that you think will be an improvement upon your existing design or process

statistically relevant
Having enough data from a test that the results

*are meaningful rather than simply the
result of chance*

multivariate testing

*Similar to A/B testing, except multiple variations in
an email are tested simultaneously, which requires
lots of data to do accurately*

Testing

106

Create a calendar or list
of tests to run.

Take the time to plan your testing to ensure that you're not only focusing your efforts on the pain points where you have the most to gain, but also that you are backing up your challenger with a solid hypothesis. Also use your calendar to help build on what you learned from previous tests.

Analytics, customer surveys and focus groups can help you identify what elements of your email program are most in need of testing and give you ideas for challenger designs and processes. Pretty much everything is open to testing, but here are some common A/B tests to get you started:

Email Design
Subject lines
- ☐ Different lengths
- ☐ Number of components (i.e., highlighting 1 offer vs. 2, etc.)
- ☐ Different offers (i.e., percent vs. dollar discount, etc.)
- ☐ Statement vs. question
- ☐ Value vs. lifestyle appeal

- ☐ First-name personalization vs. not
- ☐ Different capitalization, punctuation and special characters

Headline

- ☐ Different wording
- ☐ Different lengths
- ☐ Different sizes
- ☐ Different fonts or styling

Images

- ☐ Different sizes
- ☐ Different position
- ☐ Model vs. product
- ☐ Positioning of model (i.e., looking straight vs. looking toward key copy or call-to-action vs. looking away from it)
- ☐ Live shot vs. illustration
- ☐ Static image vs. animation
- ☐ Manufacturer image vs. your image vs. customer image

Copy

- ☐ Different position relative to images
- ☐ Different copy lengths
- ☐ Promotional vs. non-promotional copy
- ☐ Different social proof (i.e., testimonials, etc.) vs. none

Calls-to-action

- ☐ Different sizes

☐ Button vs. link

☐ Different wording

☐ Different colors

☐ Different positions

☐ Different landing pages

Product grid

☐ Number of columns in grid (i.e., 2 vs. 3 vs. 4)

☐ Which product elements to include (i.e. product name, brand, price, etc.)

Secondary messages

☐ Number of secondary messages vs. none

☐ Order of secondary messages

☐ Related to primary message vs. not

Processes

Subscription process

☐ Different signup language

☐ Different form elements (i.e., just email address vs. more required fields, etc.)

☐ Making fields optional vs. required

☐ Showing or linking to sample emails vs. not

Triggered messages

☐ How quickly to send the message after it's triggered

☐ Whether to send a series of triggered emails (i.e., 1 vs. 2 vs. 3)

Inactivity

☐ Different definition of inactive (i.e., 6 vs. 13

months of no opens or clicks)

☐ Different content tactics to reengage (i.e., rich offer, different subject lines, etc.)

☐ Different re-permission messaging

Unsubscribe process

☐ Different language on opt-out page

☐ Different alternatives made available

Testing

107

Make sure that the results of your testing are statistically relevant.

If your test groups are too small, then the results will generally not be reliable. So use large groups—of, say, several thousand active subscribers—and make sure they are randomized to ensure that the results are statistically relevant. Whether results are statistically relevant is measured in terms of confidence, with a 95% confidence that the results didn't happen by chance generally being enough to call the test complete.

Email service providers often provide at least simple testing functionality that includes confidence measures. If not, testing tool providers exist.

As a reminder, it's critical to make sure that you're using the appropriate success metrics for your test. Keep your eyes on the metrics that really matter.

Testing

108

Challenge your new champions.

Finding a new champion doesn't mean your testing is complete. Sometimes the improvements from a change are fleeting, so it's important to regularly re-test the same element or process in order to reconfirm the results or to uncover additional improvements.

The Last Word on Practice Guidelines

The Tested Rule

Because brands and their subscribers are different and sometimes face unique circumstances, there are instances where selectively, temporarily or permanently bending or breaking the Practice Guidelines will be advantageous.

Recognizing that gives us *The Tested Rule*:

Break the rules, but only if you can prove that doing so leads to superior long-term performance.

Don't break the rules just to break the rules. Do so with purpose and with your eyes wide open.

It's not difficult to find examples and case studies of brands that have broken the rules successfully, but you won't find many because usually the results just aren't that impressive. And you'll also rarely hear about the brands that broke the rules and lost.

The Last Word on Email Marketing Rules

The Evolving Rule

Books are a great way to understand the big picture of email marketing, to understand the state of the industry, and to get a firm grasp of the fundamentals. But because email marketing is a rapidly evolving channel, books are not the best way to stay up to date.

That fact brings us to *The Evolving Rule*:

Be constantly learning,

experimenting and testing

because email marketing

is always evolving.

Get ideas for your own program and current on the latest news, strategies, tactics and thought leadership by reading email marketing trade publications and industry blogs; engaging other email marketers on Twitter, LinkedIn and other online forums; and attending conferences and training programs. The email marketing community is very active, surprisingly open, and extremely welcoming. I wholeheartedly encourage you to join the conversation.

To get started, visit EmailMarketingRules.com, where I'll highlight brands that are doing it right and could be doing it better, share research and inspiration, and discuss trends affecting the email marketing industry. I hope to see you there.

Glossary

Common email marketing terms

above the fold: The portion of an email that's displayed before a subscriber scrolls

A/B testing: Sending one version of an email to a portion of your subscribers and another slightly different version to another portion of your subscribers and seeing which version performed better, often with the winning version being sent to the remainder of your list

active consent: Permission indicated when a person explicitly acts to indicate that they want you to add them to your email list (i.e., checking unchecked box); *also see* **passive consent**

***alt* text:** Text coded into an *<img>* tag that is displayed when the image is blocked and when recipients mouse over the image, although support isn't consistent

anatomy of an email: On the next page is a diagram of a basic email design, containing the most common elements. Many permutations are possible, especially within the grey portion of the diagram, which is where images tend to be used

preheader

header
navigation bar
primary message
secondary message
social media bar

footer

animated gif: An image file that displays multiple images over time

apology email: Messages sent in response to an error or mishap

back-in-stock email notification: Sent once the product is back in stock, this triggered email is sent to those who opt in on an out-of-stock product page to receive notification when that particular item is available again

below the fold: The portion of an email that's only displayed after a subscriber scrolls

best practices: Those practices that generally produce the best results or minimize risk

blacklist: A list of senders of spam typically maintained by an independent organization that is used by ISPs in determining whether and where to deliver email

blocked: When emails are not delivered by an ISP

body content or copy: The text, images and other content inside your email that becomes visible when opened

bounced: When email is rejected by an internet service provider because it was sent to an unknown email address (hard bounce) or because of a temporary condition like the recipient's mailbox being full (soft bounce)

broadcast email: An email that is sent to all subscribers

browse abandonment email: Messages that are sent to an individual subscriber in response to that person browsing certain pages of your website but not making a purchase

bulked: *see* **junked**

call-to-action (CTA): What a message asks a subscriber to do, but more specifically the buttons and links subscribers click to take action

challenger: The design or process that you think will be an improvement upon your existing design or process; *also see* **champion**

champion: Your existing design or process; *also see* **challenger**

click: When a subscriber selects a link or linked image in an email and visits the associated webpage

click reach: The percentage of your subscribers that have clicked in at least one of your emails over a period of time (i.e., over the past month or quarter)

confirmed opt-in (COI): The process of sending an email to a new subscriber that requires them to click on a link in the email to confirm their signup or else receive no additional emails

content filtering: When an ISP evaluates an email's subject line and other content as part of its process to decide whether and where the mail should be delivered

Controlling the Assault of Non-Solicited Pornography And Marketing Act of 2003 (CAN-SPAM): A law regulating commercial email messaging that forbids deceptive messaging, requires senders to include a working unsubscribe link and their mailing address in every email they send, and requires senders to honor opt-out requests quickly, among other things

conversion: When a subscriber clicks through an email and then makes a purchase, registers for an event, or takes another action requested by the email

conversion reach: The percentage of your subscribers that have converted through at least one of your emails over a period of time (i.e., over the past month or quarter)

defensive design: Design techniques that allow an email to communicate its message effectively when images are blocked

deliverability: Getting your emails delivered to your subscribers' inboxes, as opposed to blocked or junked

double opt-in: *see* **confirmed opt-in**

dynamic content: A portion of a broadcast or segmented email that is tailored to different groups of subscribers based on their geography, demographics, behavior or other factors

earned media: Marketing channels that a brand earns access to, such as word of mouth and publicity; *also see* **leased media, owned media** and **paid media**

email acquisition source: The form or mechanism through which a subscriber opts in, or the ad, sign or other vehicle that causes them to opt in

email list: All of the email addresses of your subscribers

email metrics: Measurements of the effectiveness of your email marketing program

email service provider (ESP): A commercial provider of email marketing services that allows their clients to manage their email lists, send messages, track the response of message recipients, and process opt-ins and opt-outs, among other capabilities

email template: Preformatted email file that includes all the elements you want to appear in every email, plus spots for content that changes from email to email

envelope content: The portion of an email that's visible to subscribers before they open it

expressed preferences: The topics, activities and other things that subscribers tell you they are interested in; *also see* **implied preferences**

footer: The text at the bottom of an email that includes the promotional fine print, legal language, unsubscribe link, mailing address and other details

forward to a friend (FTAF): Providing a link in your email that takes subscribers to a form that allows them to forward all or a portion of your email or a particular message promoted in your email to one or more of their friends

gift services footer: A secondary content block that is typically positioned just before the footer that pulls together links to order-by deadlines, gift guides, return policies and other important seasonal buying information

graphical text: Text that is part of an image; *also see* **HTML text**

header: The portion of an email that includes your brand's logo

hero: *see* **primary message or content block**

holiday header: A temporary header design that reflects seasonality

HTML text: Text from a limited number of fonts that are universally or widely supported across email readers; *also see* **graphical text**

image blocking: When ISPs or subscribers stop the images in an email from loading

implied preferences: The topics, activities and other things that subscribers indicate they are interested in based on their interactions with your brand; *also see* **expressed preferences**

inactive subscriber: A subscriber who has not opened or clicked in any of your emails in a long time; the opposite of an active or engaged subscriber

inactivity: When a subscriber has not opened or clicked in any of your emails in a long time

internet service provider (ISP): Shorthand term for providers of web-based, desktop and mobile email inboxes that send, store and organize messages for users and manage and block spam (i.e., Gmail, Outlook, etc.)

junked: When emails are routed to a recipient's "junk" or "spam" folder by an ISP

landing page: Webpage that subscribers are

directed to when they click on a call-to-action in one of your emails

leased media: Marketing channels that a brand has free access to but doesn't control, such as Facebook, Twitter and Pinterest; *also see* **earned media**, **owned media** and **paid media**

list building: The process of adding email addresses to your mailing list

list churn: Subscribers lost to unsubscribes, spam complaints and bounces from email addresses that no longer work

list rental: Having a message sent on your behalf to an email list owned by someone else

live content: Images and other email content that vary based on when the email is opened, what kind of device it's opened on, and other factors

multivariate testing: Similar to A/B testing, except multiple variations in an email are tested simultaneously, which requires lots of data to do accurately

navigation bar: A row of links to important pages on your website

open: When a subscriber views an email with images enabled

open reach: The percentage of your subscribers that have opened at least one of your emails over a period of time (i.e., over the past month or quarter)

opt down: Allowing subscribers to choose to receive your emails less frequently

opt-in confirmation page: Webpage or messaging that follows a successful email signup

opt-in email marketing: Sending email only to those who have given you permission to do so; *also see* **opt-out email marketing**

opt-out email marketing: Sending email to those who have not given you permission to do so and requiring them to unsubscribe or mark your emails as spam if they don't want to receive future emails; *also see* **opt-in email marketing**

opt-out page: *see* **unsubscribe page**

opt-out process: *see* **unsubscribe process**

opt over: Giving subscribers the option to opt into one of your other channels, such as social or mobile, during your email unsubscribe process

owned media: Marketing channels that a brand owns, such as their website, blog and mobile app; *also see* **earned media**, **leased media** and **paid media**

paid media: Marketing channels that a brand pays to have access to, such as TV, radio, magazines, newspapers, billboards, paid search and display ads; *also see* **earned media**, **leased media** and **owned media**

passive consent: Permission indicated when a person does not act to keep you from adding them to your email list (i.e., not unchecking pre-checked box); *also see* **active consent**

permission: Actively or passively agreeing to receive promotional email

personalization: Including information that's unique to the recipient in the subject line or body copy of an email

preference center: Webpage that displays a subscriber's email address and other details, such as profile information (zip code, etc.) and communication preferences (topics of interest, etc.), and allows them to make changes as well as unsubscribe

preheader text: HTML text positioned at the very top of an email that is most often used to reinforce or extend the subject line

primary message: The main message of an email, which is usually positioned at the top of the email and larger than other messages in the email

product grid: A multi-column and usually multi-row layout where each grid cell contains a product image and other information such as product name, brand and price

progressive profiling: Collecting additional demographic data and information about interests from subscribers by periodically asking them questions via email

quality assurance: Ensuring that email content is error-free and functions properly and that the intended subscribers receive that content at the intended time

reactivate: Getting a subscriber to open or click one of your emails after a long period of having not done so

recovery module: A multi-column secondary content block, usually positioned right before the footer, that contains many links to different product categories, brands or other areas of your website that is designed to appeal to subscribers who were uninterested in the other calls-to-action in the email

reengagement email: *see* **win-back email**

relevance: How valuable a subscriber thinks your emails are over time—which is largely determined by how many emails you send, when they arrive, their content, and how they look and function within whichever email reader is being used

rendering: How an email reader translates an email's coding and displays the email

re-permission email: Messages that ask a subscriber to reconfirm their subscription by clicking on a link in the email in order to remain on your active mailing list

seasonality: Related to an upcoming or current season, holiday or buying occasion

secondary message: The other message(s) in an email, usually following and smaller than the primary message

secondary navigation bar: A second nav bar that sits right under your standard nav bar that typically provides deeper navigation into one of your standard nav bar links, provides links to seasonal merchandise and content, or provides links that support the primary message or theme of the email

segmentation: Sending a particular message to only those subscribers who are likely to respond based on their geography, demographics, behavior or other factors; or sending the same message to subscribers at different times based on their time zone or geography

sender name: The name that appears in the "From" line in an email reader

sender reputation: A reflection of your trustworthiness as an email source that is affected by spam complaint rates and other factors that internet service providers use to determine whether to deliver, junk or block your email

share with your network (SWYN): Functionality that allows subscribers to add content from your email to their social media timeline so their friends can see it

shopping cart abandonment email: Messages that are sent to an individual subscriber in response to that person leaving one or more items in their shopping cart

snippet text: A portion of the first text from inside the email that some email readers display after the subject line in the inbox, when highlighting a new email's arrival, or in other situations; *also see* **preheader text**

social media bar: A row of social media icons that

link to your brand's pages on those social media sites

spam: Any email that recipients consider unwanted or irrelevant—even if it's from brands they know and even if they gave the brand permission to email them

spamtrap or honeypot: Sending email to these long-abandoned or uncirculated email addresses causes ISPs to label you a spammer and block your email

split testing: *see* **A/B testing**

statistically relevant: Having enough data from a test that the results are meaningful rather than simply the result of chance

subject line: The text that appears in the "Subject" line in an email reader

subscriber: Someone who has consented to joining your email list

subscriber lifetime value: The cumulative revenue generated by a subscriber during their time on your list

swipe file: A record of your top-performing subject lines, emails and landing pages that you return to for learnings and inspiration

system text: *see* **HTML text**

targeting: Sending the right message to the right subscriber at the right time

win-back email: Messages that are sent to an individual subscriber in response to that person having not engaged with your emails or made a purchase in a long time in an effort to get them to engage and make a purchase again

Let's keep the conversation going. Please visit EmailMarketingRules.com:

- Real-world examples of the practices discussed in this book
- Exclusive email marketing research
- Tips and inspiration to help you improve your program
- Insights into the trends affecting the email marketing industry